The Story of Science

Anna Claybourne

Illustrated by Adam Larkum

Designed by Steve Wood

Edited by Jane Chisholm

Scientific consultant: Dr. Patricia Fara,
University of Cambridge

Cover design by Ian McNee

Additional material by Alex Frith and Dr. Lisa Jane Gillespie

Contents

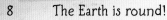

The discoveries that have helped us to understand the Earth, our humble home planet.

Our place in space

Look far beyond Earth into the blackness of space, to discover stars, planets, galaxies, black holes and more.

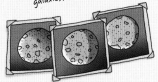

Physics

The strange science of matter and energy – what makes heat, why things float, what's the speed of light, and whether an apple really fell on Newton's head.

Chemistry

All about what stuff is really made of, and how chemicals react – sometimes with a loud bang!

The
Story
of
Science

Note on dates

Some very old dates in this book are marked "BC", which means "Before Christ". The year is counted backwards roughly from the year of Christ's birth. BC is sometimes known as "BCE", meaning "Before Common Era". If a date has a "c." before it, it stands for "circa", which is Latin for "around". This means that the event happened around this time - no one is sure of the exact date.

Internet links

There are lots of websites with information about great scientists and scientific discoveries. Some have exciting interactive games and quizzes for you to try as well. At the Usborne Quicklinks website, you'll find links to some great sites where you can find out more about hundreds of amazing scientists and discoveries, see pictures and animations, look up all kinds of science facts, and learn how to do your own scientific experiments.

For links to these sites, go to the Usborne Quicklinks website at www.usborne.com/quicklinks and enter the keywords "Story of Science". When using the Internet, please follow the Internet safety guidelines shown on the Usborne Quicklinks website. The links at Usborne Quicklinks are regularly reviewed and updated, but Usborne Publishing is not responsible for and does not accept liability for the content on any website other than its own. We recommend that children are supervised while using the Internet.

Numbers and counting

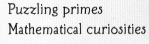

Living things

Our planet is the only one we know that has things living on it! Read about some amazing discoveries to do with life on Earth.

The human body

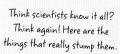

The amazing science of how your body works, what can go wrong, and how to fix it.

Prehistoric finds

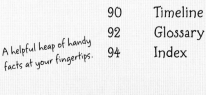

Find out what scientists have found out by digging things up from long, long ago.

Think scientists know it all? Think again! Here are the things that really stump them.

A helpful heap of handy facts at your fingertips.

What is science?

The word "science" simply means "knowledge". Scientists try to find out about things and how they work. That can mean anything at all – digging up fossils or discovering stars; learning how animals talk; measuring the distance to the moon; or even finding out how our own brains think.

Finding things out

Have you ever messed around with something just to see what would happen? Humans have a natural urge to try to understand and discover things. So, over thousands of years, science has become a big part of our lives. We just can't stop trying to find out more, and more, and more...

> Science is what you know.

> Science is organized knowledge.

> Science is facts. Just as houses are made of stones, so science is made of facts.

These great scientists and thinkers all had something to say about exactly what science is.

Bertrand Russell   **Herbert Spencer**   **Henri Poincaré**

Experiments

Science involves a lot of experiments – tests that help us find out about things. To make sure the results are right, scientists must design their experiments carefully, repeat them several times and keep written records.

> Hmm – what happens if I put an egg in the fire?

> Yum!

Early people found out useful things by experimenting.

What is science for?

Science is amazingly useful. When we find out new facts, such as what causes a particular disease, it helps us to invent new things, such as vaccines and medicines.

But science doesn't always need a practical purpose. Scientists are still interested in finding things out for the sake of it, even if they might never be useful. Where will it lead us? We don't know.

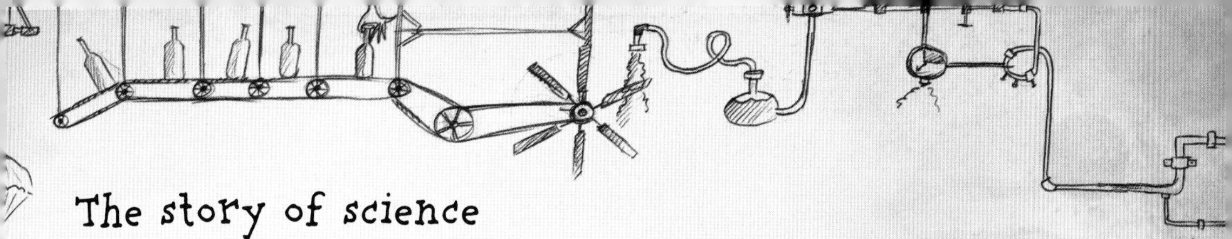

The story of science

This book explores many of the greatest moments in the history of science. Here are a few of the times when science took centre stage:

6,000 years ago

Ancient civilizations begin writing down scientific discoveries.

500 to 1200

Baghdad, now Iraq's capital, is a great centre of science.

1700s

The Enlightenment – a great boom in scientific study – happens in Europe.

Today

Scientists all over the world work in universities or for big companies.

What is a scientist?

Today, the word "scientist" means someone who does scientific experiments to find out about the world around us. However, this word wasn't invented until 1833, when English science writer William Whewell invented it to describe someone who studies nature.

Before that, people who studied science were often known as "natural philosophers". Or they were called naturalists, chemists and so on, depending on what they studied. Today, there are hundreds of types of scientists. You can find some of them in the glossary on page 92.

> Man is the interpreter of nature, science the right interpretation.

William Whewell

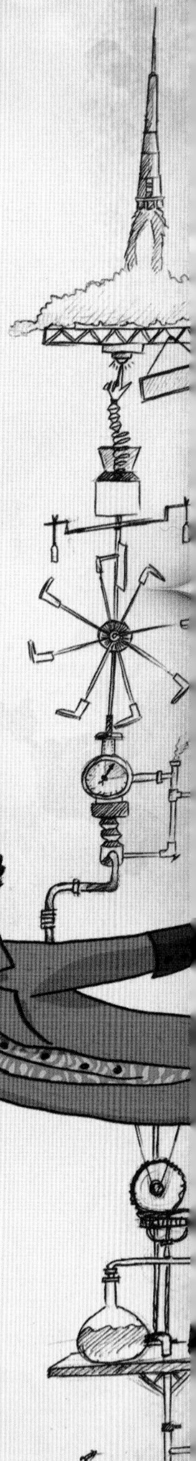

Are you a scientist?

Very important scientific discoveries are sometimes rewarded with a Nobel Prize.

Any time you experiment with something to find out how it works, you're doing a kind of science. If you're always taking things apart, or if you're fascinated by fire, space, spiders or machines – or anything else – you could make a great scientist!

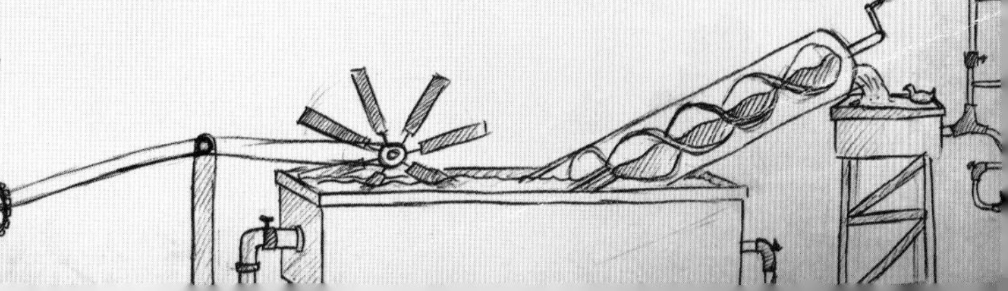

Looks flat to me!

Many early people lived on fertile plains where it was easy to grow crops. So the world probably did seem like a flat disk, surrounded by hills or seas.

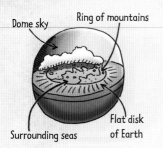

Dome sky   Ring of mountains

Flat disk of Earth

Surrounding seas

The Earth is round!

As you probably know, our planet, the Earth, is a giant sphere. No one falls off because Earth's powerful gravity pulls us towards it, wherever we are on its surface. But a long time ago, such an idea wouldn't have made any sense to most people. They thought the Earth was flat.

The flat Earth

Many early people, such as the Sumerians and the ancient Egyptians, saw the Earth as a giant flat disk (or, for the ancient Chinese, a square). They thought the sky must be a huge dome, with the stars, Sun and moon attached to it. No one was sure what lay at the "edges", because in those days people rarely moved long distances.

Could it be round?

However, around 2,400 years ago, the ancient Greeks began to question this idea. The great Greek thinker Aristotle, for example, saw various things that suggested the Earth was actually a ball floating in space.

How Eratosthenes measured the Earth

Eratosthenes didn't have a giant tape measure, so how did he measure the Earth?

He knew that in Syene in Egypt, in the middle of summer, the Sun was right overhead, and a stick stuck in the ground would cast no shadow.

Alexandria (shadow)   Syene (no shadow)

7°

800 km (500 miles)

At Alexandria, about 800km (500 miles) north, there were shadows. By measuring them, Eratosthenes could tell how much the Earth must curve between the two cities.

From this segment, he could calculate the size of the whole Earth.

7°

As ships sail away, they disappear over the Earth's curved surface...

Earth's shadow

...and at a lunar eclipse, the Earth always casts a round shadow on the moon.

The Earth MUST be a ball!

A later Greek, Eratosthenes, agreed that the Earth was a sphere, and decided to measure it. His results were very close to our modern measurements, which show that the Earth has a circumference of about 40,000km (25,000 miles).

Ideas and arguments

By medieval times, almost everyone agreed that the Earth was a sphere. But a few didn't. Some Christians didn't want to believe the world could be round, as the Bible said it had "four corners". Others worried that if the Earth was a ball, you could fall off it. They wondered if people could possibly live on the other side of the Earth, and what they might be like.

Of course, one problem was that the Earth was so big, no one had ever explored all of it to find out its shape once and for all. But that was about to change.

Around the world

During the 1400s, Europeans began to explore more and more of the world. One of them, Italian-born Christopher Columbus, set off west across the Atlantic Ocean in 1492. He was hoping to sail right around the world to eastern lands such as China – but he didn't manage to, as America was in the way.

But not long afterwards, in 1519, Portuguese explorer Ferdinand Magellan led an expedition that did complete a journey around the world. Other explorers pieced together more and more of the planet, and people began to make realistic world maps and globes.

The first pictures

By the time spaceflight began in the 1950s, it was obvious that the Earth was a sphere. But it was still amazing to see the first ever photographs of the Earth from a distance. Russian astronaut Aleksei Leonov described the view of Earth from space like this:

Some writers imagined that the people living on the opposite side of the world from them must be strange, monstrous beings.

Flat-Earthers

Someone who believes the Earth is flat is known as a "Flat-Earther". Despite the evidence for a round Earth, English writer Samuel Rowbotham started a new Flat-Earth movement in 1849 to promote this outdated belief.

Sun

This flat-Earth map from 1931 shows a flat disk with the North Pole in the middle and a ring of icy mountains around the edge.

The Earth was small, light blue, and so touchingly alone... I believe I never knew what the word "round" meant until I saw Earth from space.

9

The age of the Earth

Compared to a human life, or even the whole of human history, our planet is very, very, very old. But how old? The answer lies in the Earth's rocks.

How rock forms

Scientists now think that rock can form in three main ways.

Sedimentary rock forms when mud and silt collect and harden – often on the seabed.

Igneous rock forms when hot molten rock from deep inside the Earth cools and hardens.

Metamorphic rock forms when other rocks are squeezed or heated in the Earth.

Stone seashells and stripy rocks

Around 1,000 years ago, a Chinese thinker named Shen Kuo was among the first to suggest how rocks might be made. He saw that they were often striped, and contained shapes that looked like stone animals (which we now call fossils). Shen Kuo realized that rocks could have formed as layers of sand and mud settled on to the seabed.

This layer of mountain rock is full of seashells...

...so it must once have been part of the sea.

According to Steno (see right), rock formed in flat layers, or "strata" – the oldest were always at the bottom.

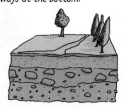

Later, rock might change position or shape, but it had still started as flat layers.

Stone sharks' teeth

In the 1600s, Dutch natural philosopher Niels Stensen – known as Steno – came up with the same idea. People often found fossils known as "tongue stones", which looked like big sharks' teeth. Some said they fell from the sky, or grew inside rocks.

But Steno was sure they came from real shark teeth. They must have fallen to the bottom of the sea, and been covered in layers of mud. The mud had hardened into rock. Then it had somehow been lifted up out of the sea.

As old as the hills

If rock really did form this way, the process must have taken ages. In fact, it must have taken millions of years.

But, in the 1600s, most people in Europe believed religious teachings about how old the Earth was – and this caused a problem. From studying the Bible, Christians estimated that the Earth was only about 6,000 years old.

The more people studied rocks, however, the more they realized the Earth had to be older than that.

A new discovery

The Earth seemed to be much older than people had once thought, but scientists couldn't agree just how old it was (see box). Then, in 1896, French physicist Henri Becquerel discovered radioactivity (see page 46). Soon afterwards, in the early 1900s, Ernest Rutherford and Bertram Boltwood developed radiometric dating – a way of using radioactivity to measure the age of rocks. Some rocks contain radioactive minerals that give out energy over time, changing the chemicals in the rock in a way that can be measured.

In the 1950s, using this method, scientists agreed that the Earth was about 4.55 billion years old.

Scientists use a machine called a mass spectrometer to find out exactly what chemicals a rock is made of, and how old it must be.

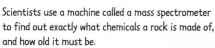

Oooh, it's even older than me!

How old?

In the 1700s and 1800s, Scottish geologists James Hutton and Charles Lyell said that rocks were constantly being worn away and forming again, in a huge cycle.

Around 1800, English geologist William Smith showed that there were different fossils in different rock layers. This suggested that animal life had been changing for millions of years.

Through the 1800s, many scientists made their own calculations of the age of the Earth. Based on how long rocks must have taken to form, their estimates ranged from millions to billions of years.

3 billion!

1.5 billion!

100 million!

In fact, scientists now think the Earth is even older than this – 4.55 billion (4,500,000,000) years old.

Jigsaw Earth

Ferdinand Magellan was the first to lead a sailing expedition around the world.

Have you ever noticed that on a map of the world, some of the continents look as if they could fit together, like jigsaw pieces? Well, millions of years ago, they did.

Puzzle pieces

The shapes of the continents only became clear to us from the 1500s, as explorers began to sail the world, making measurements as they went.

People first spotted these "jigsaw pieces" about 400 years ago. In the 1500s, explorers such as Ferdinand Magellan began to sail around the world, and the first reasonably accurate world maps were made. They showed that some coastlines, especially those of Africa and South America, had strangely similar shapes. In 1596, Belgian map-maker Abraham Ortelius remarked on their jigsaw-like fit.

The vestiges of the rupture reveal themselves... the projecting parts of Europe and Africa... the recesses of America.

Abraham Ortelius saw that the two sides of the Atlantic Ocean matched, as if they had once been a whole piece that had "ruptured" or broken apart.

Wegener's world

Mesosaurus, a water reptile dating from about 225 million years ago, was one of the fossils found on both sides of the Atlantic.

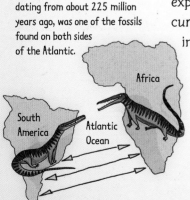

In 1911, Alfred Wegener, a German explorer and weather expert, noticed another mysterious match. Besides the curious coastlines, some of the same fossils were found in eastern South America and West Africa, suggesting that they were once joined. Mountain ranges and coal deposits also matched up across the gap.

Wegener thought the continents had separated slowly over time, in a process he called "continental drift". He said they must have been joined together in a single, huge land mass, which he named "Pangaea".

How did it happen?

Wegener's ideas weren't taken very seriously at first, as it was hard to see how the continents could have drifted so far. But, in the 1950s, some new discoveries made sense of what he had said.

Firstly, US geologist Maurice Ewing discovered a huge system of volcanic undersea mountain ridges running beneath all the world's oceans. Meanwhile, another American scientist, Harry Hess, found that the rocks of the seabed were much younger than rocks on land.

Hess realized that, as molten rock poured out of the undersea ridges, it formed a new seabed. This spread out, pushing apart the continents on either side. Over millions of years, the continents had moved around the globe.

The plates of Pangaea

But, if new seabed was being formed, why wasn't the Earth getting bigger? Hess and other scientists saw that as new seabed formed in some areas, it disappeared in others, by plunging into deep ocean trenches where one section of the Earth's crust slid underneath another. The huge, shifting sections of crust became known as tectonic plates.

By studying tectonic plates, rocks, fossils and earthforms around the world, scientists have now been able to work out how "Pangaea" might have looked, and how the continents have separated and moved over time.

This shows how hot molten rock flows out from inside the Earth at an undersea ridge. It cools into solid rock and pushes the ridge apart, creating new seabed.

Crumple zones

As the continents move, they sometimes push into each other, making the land buckle and fold upwards to form mountains.

India, for example, crashed into the rest of Asia about 60 million years ago, pushing the land up to create the world's highest mountain range, the Himalayas. The world's continents are still moving, and the Himalayas are still rising – by about 5mm (0.2 inches) per year.

225 million years ago

65 million years ago

Present day

Freezing and frying

Since the Earth formed, the whole planet has changed its temperature many times. There have been many freezing cold ice ages, with much hotter times in between. The first clues about how this happened were in icy mountains...

1760 River of ice

A mine in the mountains of Grindelwald, in Switzerland, had to close in 1760 when a flood of ice flowed over it. Geologists began to study glaciers – huge icepacks that collect on mountains, then flow downhill like rivers.

This gravel is a deposit left behind by gigantic glaciers.

Valley carved out by a glacier

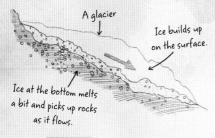

A glacier

Ice builds up on the surface.

Ice at the bottom melts a bit and picks up rocks as it flows.

1840 Rock-solid evidence

Swiss-American Louis Agassiz studied rock formations in Switzerland and Britain. He saw that they were shaped by glaciers that had once covered both countries – a time he described as an "ice age".

1896 Warming up the Earth

So what had made the Earth get warmer? In 1896, Swedish chemist Svante Arrhenius found that carbon dioxide (CO_2) traps heat. He suggested that when there is more of it in the atmosphere, the Earth warms up.

Heat radiation from the Sun hits the Earth, then bounces back into space. (Some of the heat is deflected by clouds.)

Factories and power stations generate carbon dioxide and other gases that trap heat, now known as "greenhouse gases".

Carbon dioxide in the atmosphere reflects some of the heat, keeping the air warmer for longer.

1920

Serbian astronomer Milutin Milankovitch found another cause for the Earth's changing temperature. He saw that the Earth's orbit around the Sun shifted in regular patterns. It made sense that when the orbit was closer to the Sun, the planet would be warmer.

Hey! I thought of that in 1875.

Scotsman James Croll had written about the same idea, but he was ignored at the time.

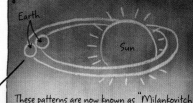

Earth

Sun

These patterns are now known as "Milankovitch cycles". The difference in the amount of heat radiation from the Sun causes ice ages every 100,000 years.

Heat history

Scientists knew that the Earth had been both much colder and hotter in the past, but when did all these changes take place? These scientists helped to find the answers...

1957

Italian Cesare Emiliani collected fossils of ancient sea creatures. The chemicals they were made of showed how hot or cold the Earth was when the creatures were alive.

Really cold... warm...cold again... hot hot hot!.. cold again...

1973

Briton Nick Shackleton studied cores drilled from glaciers and from the ocean floor. He found patterns in them that proved that the Milankovitch cycles matched with the coldest periods — or ice ages — in the Earth's history.

Shackleton tested air bubbles trapped in the ice to measure carbon dioxide levels in the past.

1991

American geologists James Kennett and Lowell Stott examined ancient plant seeds from the bottom of the Antarctic ocean. They discovered that 55 million years ago, the Earth was so hot that many living things died out.

1996 A great flood?

All over the world, people tell stories about a great flood in the distant past. US geologists William Ryan and Walter Pitman uncovered hard evidence for such a flood in the Black Sea.

Run away! Run away!

What's the rush?

Fossils showed that it had once been full of freshwater fish. But around 7,500 years ago, in just a few years, it grew much bigger, and was filled with saltwater animals. Studies like this suggest that a hot period melted glaciers and made sea levels rise fast, pouring salt water across the land.

Today It's all our fault!

Arrhenius was right that greenhouse gases warm the Earth, but he thought warmer weather would be a good thing. Scientists all over the world have now found signs that the Earth is getting too hot too quickly, and that this could damage many species, including our own.

Carbon dioxide and other greenhouse gases come from power stations, cars, planes and even cows.

Trees, which soak up carbon dioxide, are cut down all the time, often to make room for more cows, roads and power stations.

As long as 6,000 years ago, houses in Banpo, China, were built to line up with the constellation Yingshi (Pegasus in English) when it was overhead, probably for good luck.

Stars and galaxies

Studying the stars is one of the oldest types of science there is. Many ancient peoples tracked the stars and gave them names. But how did we find out what stars really are?

Patterns and shapes

Many ancient people noticed that although the stars seemed to move, they stayed in a fixed pattern. Some groups of stars formed familiar shapes, such as a cross or a zigzag, which we now call constellations. In some early societies, constellations were seen as holy beings or good luck signs.

People also used the positions of the stars to find their way. The North Star, for example, guides people north, and was also used to lay out the Egyptian pyramids.

Seeing patterns

The stars in a constellation look close together, but they aren't. Some may be much further away from the Earth than others. But viewed from the Earth, they line up and form a pattern. We spot these patterns in the stars because when we look at random dots, our brains automatically try to find familiar shapes

Alkaid -101 light years away

Mizar - 78 light years away

The Plough or Big Dipper constellation

Naming the stars

In about 1400 BC, the ancient Mesopotamians, who lived in the area that is now Iraq, created a list of facts about astronomy called the Mul.Apin. Written on clay tablets, it named 66 stars and constellations.

The ancient Greeks also named many stars, and so did Arabic astronomers based in the city of Baghdad about 1,000 years ago. Most of the star names we use today come from Arabic versions of Greek names.

Most of the stars in the constellation Orion (the Hunter) have Arabic names.

Bellatrix is Latin for "female warrior"

Betelgeuse (from the Arabic for "warrior's hand")

Alnitak ("girdle")

Alnilam ("string of pearls")

Saiph ("sword")

Mintaka ("belt")

Rigel (from Arabic Rijl, "foot")

Where are the stars?

Many ancient peoples thought stars were lights fixed to a giant rotating dome or sphere around the Earth. This meant the stars must all be quite close to the Earth.

Faraway stars

But one ancient Greek thinker, Democritus, had other ideas. He said that the stars were all suns, similar to our Sun, but scattered far and wide. He also said that the band of light visible in the night sky – now known as our galaxy, the Milky Way – was made up of faraway stars.

What stars really are

Over 2,000 years later, scientists found that Democritus was right – stars were all balls of gas at different distances.

First, in 1832, German astronomer Friedrich Bessel calculated the distance to the star 61 Cygni using a method called stellar parallax (see box). After this, using the latest telescopes, astronomers began to study the stars more closely than ever. They found that stars came in many sizes and colours, all different distances from Earth.

Studies of our Sun's light showed that the Sun was made of burning gases. Stars gave out the same kinds of light as the Sun, showing they must be made of burning gases too. By comparing them, scientists could find out which gases stars were made of and how hot they were. In the early 1900s, astronomers documented many thousands of stars, classifying them by their temperature.

Galaxies galore

A galaxy is a vast cluster of stars. While studying our home galaxy, the Milky Way, scientists saw strange shapes that looked like other galaxies. In about 1923, using a new telescope, US astronomer Edwin Hubble proved that there were indeed many other galaxies beyond our own.

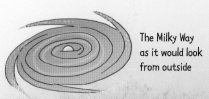

The Milky Way as it would look from outside

61 Cygni is actually a "double star" made up of 2 stars very close together.

Ooooh...

Friedrich Bessel

61 Cygni was the first star to have its distance from Earth measured. Friedrich Bessel found that it was 11 light years away (the distance light travels in 11 years).

Stellar parallax

Parallax means the way things seem to move when we change our position. As the Earth orbits the Sun, we see stars from slightly different angles. They appear to move very slightly, and from this we can calculate their distance.

As the Earth moves, this star will appear to move more than the stars further away.

←Star

Earth→○   ○:← Sun ○

Parallax movements are tiny and can only be seen with a telescope.

The Milky Way galaxy is shaped like a giant, swirling disk of stars. This makes a band of starlight appear where the stars of the Milky Way are thickest.

Jupiter

Earth

Venus

Mars

Mercury

Sun

The planets are found at various distances from the Sun. Mercury is the closest.

The Solar System

Our Sun is just one of the trillions of stars in the universe. It has several planets, asteroids and other objects orbiting around it. Together, these are known as the Solar System.

Ancient astronomy

The ancient Sumerians, who lived in what is now Iraq, were among the earliest astronomers.

The Sumerians were studying the night sky as long as 5,500 years ago. This Sumerian clay tablet image, showing in the background the Sun surrounded by planets and stars, is about 4,500 years old.

William Herschel

I have looked further into space than any human being did before me.

Discovering the planets

Ancient people realized that while most stars stayed in a fixed pattern, a few seemed to move around the sky. The ancient Greeks named these moving objects the *planetes*, or "wanderers". Scientists now know that they are not stars, but balls of rock and gas orbiting (circling) the Sun.

The five planets

Ancient astronomers knew of five planets (not including Earth). They were Mercury, Venus, Mars, Jupiter and Saturn – the planets that we can see without a telescope. In those days, people thought the planets were orbiting around the Earth, not the Sun. Some thought they were their gods, moving through the skies. All the planets we know today, except Earth, are named after ancient gods.

New planets

After telescopes were invented in the early 1600s, more objects became visible in space. In 1781, British astronomer William Herschel discovered what he thought was a new star, but later realized was a planet. This new planet was eventually named Uranus. The orbit of Uranus showed that there must be another planet nearby, whose gravity was pulling on it. Scientists searched the skies until, in 1846, they found another new planet, Neptune.

Saturn

Uranus

Neptune

The solar system is about 13 billion km (8 billion miles) across.

Pluto

There were lots of ideas for a name for the new planet. "Pluto" was suggested by an 11-year-old British girl, Venetia Burney. She loved mythology, and chose the name of the Roman god of the underworld for the dark, icy planet.

A ninth planet?

In 1930, a US astronomer named Clyde Tombaugh was searching for new planets in the solar system. And he found one! The tiny new planet was named Pluto.

But, around 2000, more small planet-like objects were found, and scientists began to argue about what counted as a planet. In 2006, they agreed that small planets like Pluto were not true planets but "dwarf planets". So today, the solar system has just eight main planets, including Earth.

Life on other planets?

William Herschel, who discovered Uranus, believed that the planets and the Sun were home to living beings. And in the early 1900s, some astronomers thought they could see canals on Mars. But space probes have now visited the planets, and have so far found no definite signs of life.

Moons and rings

In 1610, using the newly invented telescope, the Italian astronomer Galileo discovered that Jupiter had four moons orbiting it. He also saw that Saturn had strange ear-like parts, later found to be rings of dust and ice.

Io, one of Jupiter's moons

Over the centuries, astronomers have found that Jupiter, Uranus and Neptune have rings too – and that most of the planets have moons. Saturn has at least 60 and Jupiter has over 63!

In 1997, the rover *Sojourner* became the first robot to explore of Mars. A fourth rover, *Curiousity*, began exploring Mars in 2012.

Planets galore

In the mid-1990s, astronomers found that some other stars, beyond our Solar System, have planets orbiting them too. Since then, hundreds of these "extrasolar" planets have been spotted. Some of them are similar to Earth, and may even have the right conditions for life to exist.

Welcome, Earthlings!

There it goes again!

Round and round...

Same as yesterday!

The Earth moves!

People once thought the Earth was the centre of the universe, with the Sun, planets and stars circling around it. They were wrong – but it took many years to prove it.

The Sun's path

The Sun seems to travel across the sky each day, so you can see why people thought it orbited the Earth. One ancient Greek philosopher, Aristarchus, did suggest that Earth and the other planets actually moved around the Sun. But, in the 2nd century, when another philosopher, Ptolemy, claimed the Earth stood still, most people believed him.

Going backwards

But there was still a puzzle for astronomers. As the planets moved across the sky, they sometimes seemed to change direction and go backwards for a while. Ptolemy explained this by saying they moved in complex patterns.

But, in the early 1500s, a Polish astronomer, Nicolaus Copernicus, studied this backwards movement again. He saw that it made sense if the planets and the Earth all moved around the Sun. As the Earth zoomed past a slower planet, that planet would appear to us to go into reverse.

In 1543, the year he died, Copernicus published a book claiming the Earth and planets did orbit the Sun after all.

Ptolemy's model

Ptolemy said that the Earth was a round ball, with the planets and Sun orbiting around it in perfect circles. Beyond them were the stars, which also revolved around the Earth in a neat pattern.

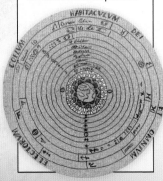

Copernicus's system, shown here, put the Sun in the middle. All the planets, including the Earth, orbited in circles around it. This idea is known as "heliocentricity", from the Greek *helios* meaning Sun, and *kentros* meaning middle.

The Earth moves around the Sun once a year.

Day and night happen because the Earth itself is spinning.

As the Earth spins, the Sun appears to move across the sky.

Was Copernicus right?

Some religious leaders didn't like Copernicus's work. Church teachings said that space was a perfect creation that could never change, with the Earth in the middle.

So in 1572, when Danish astronomer Tycho Brahe saw a new star, it caused a big stir. It proved that the heavens *could* change. Then, Brahe's assistant Johannes Kepler found evidence that the planets moved in oval orbits around the Sun. More and more astronomers were realizing that Copernicus's heliocentric model was right.

Galileo's telescope

Around 1609, the invention of the first telescope shook up the study of space. It was actually designed for use in battle, but Italian astronomer Galileo Galilei built his own version for studying the sky. When he spotted four moons orbiting the planet Jupiter, it was proof, at last, that not everything in space orbited the Earth.

The truth on trial

Like Copernicus and Kepler, Galileo saw that the patterns the planets made in the sky meant they orbited the Sun. But some representatives of the Catholic Church said this was heresy (meaning you could get into trouble for believing it).

In 1633, after writing a book supporting Copernicus, Galileo was put on trial. He was forced to say he was mistaken, and that the Earth stood still. But, as he left the courtroom, Galileo is said to have muttered under his breath: "And yet it does move."

Before long, the scientific evidence was widely accepted, and the Church had to change its story.

The constellation of Cassiopeia

The star Tycho saw was a supernova – an old star exploding. It shone for a few months before disappearing.

Sketches of the sky

Galileo drew pictures of the things he saw with his telescope. They included the moons of Jupiter...

...details of Earth's moon...

...and Saturn's rings, which Galileo called its "ears".

And yet it *does* move...

What did you say?

It's even bigger than I thought!

The universe is so huge, it's almost impossible to imagine. It contains trillions of stars and planets.

The story of the universe

The word "universe" means everything there is – our world, all the other planets and stars, all of space, and all of time. But where did the universe come from?

Seeing stars

People have always been able to see lots of stars in the sky at night. But, ever since telescopes were invented, we have been able to see even more of them. As telescopes improved, astronomers could see further and further out into space. In fact, it seemed to go on forever. Scientists still can't be sure whether the universe really is infinite (endless and everlasting), or whether it has a shape, a size, a beginning and an end. But they do have some ideas.

Getting bigger

In the 1920s, astronomer Edwin Hubble discovered that there were galaxies beyond our own (see page 17), and began studying them. By about 1929, he had found that the other galaxies he could see were moving away from us. The further away they were, the faster they were going.

This must mean that all the parts of the universe were once much closer together than they are now. In 1931, a Belgian scientist, Georges Lemaître, claimed that all the matter in the universe had once been packed together in a solid ball, a "Primeval Atom", and had expanded outwards from there.

Look back in time

Light takes time to travel through space. In a year, it travels about 9.5 million million km (known as a light year). When we look at a faraway space object, such as a galaxy, that is 3 million light years away, we are actually seeing light that left that galaxy 3 million years ago. In effect, we are looking back in time. By studying very faraway objects, astronomers can observe events from the history of the universe.

This is the Triangulum galaxy, which is 3 million light years from Earth.

Edwin Hubble made his discoveries using a newly built telescope at the Mount Wilson Observatory in California, USA.

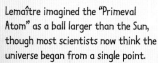

Lemaître imagined the "Primeval Atom" as a ball larger than the Sun, though most scientists now think the universe began from a single point.

The Big Bang

Several other scientists began working with Lemaître's ideas, calculating how the "Primeval Atom" could have exploded to create all the stars, planets and galaxies we can see now. But British astronomer Fred Hoyle didn't think much of this approach. In 1950 he dismissed the idea of an explosion as nonsense, rudely calling it a "Big Bang".

Then, in the 1960s, scientists detected a low level of radio wave energy bouncing around in space. This fitted with the idea of the "Big Bang", as the explosion would have created exactly this kind of energy. Soon, most astronomers began to accept that the Big Bang was the best explanation for the start of the universe – and the nickname stuck. If it did happen, scientists have calculated that the universe must now be about 13.7 billion years old.

Of course there was no Big Bang!

Fred Hoyle

BANG!!!

Er, apart from that one.

Black holes

A black hole is a space object that has a lot of matter in an incredibly small volume. This gives it very strong gravity that sucks in everything close to it, even light. Black holes look dark, as light can't escape from them, but we can detect them by the way their gravity pulls on nearby space dust and stars.

Black holes were first described in 1783 by English astronomer John Michell. But they weren't named "black holes" until 1967.

Mysteries of the universe

But if the universe had a beginning, what was there before? What is outside it, and when will it end? Some scientists say that one day the universe could shrink back to nothing, in a "Big Crunch", or keep expanding for ever.

Others think that instead of starting with a Big Bang, the universe goes through an endless cycle of expanding and shrinking. Some have even said that there could be a "multiverse", made up of many different universes, perhaps connected by black holes.

The story continues...

Of course, as we cannot step outside our universe to look at it, it's very hard to find out the truth. Scientists are still debating these mysteries and coming up with new ideas.

Some scientists claim that the universe is not ball-shaped, but is more like a ring or a tube.

Torus-shaped (ring-shaped) universe

The moon

People have always been fascinated by the moon. They've invented stories about it, studied it through telescopes and, eventually, launched missions to visit and investigate it.

3,000 years ago Ancient cultures

Come to my party the day after the next full moon - see you there!

The ancient Greeks believed the goddess Selene lit up the moon with her glowing crown. They used the moon to measure time. A month was the number of days taken for the full moon to disappear and reappear.

2,000 years ago Moon myths

Some Asian cultures saw a rabbit in the shapes on the face of the moon and invented stories about it.

c. 445 BC Rock and light

Most people believed the moon gave out its own light. But one Greek philosopher, Anaxagoras, suggested that it was just a lump of rock that reflected the light from the Sun.

It reflects the light like a mirror.

c. 300 BC   ...and 1687
Changing tides

Aristotle knew there was a connection between the moon and changing sea levels. Much later, Isaac Newton applied his theory of gravity to tides. He realized that they were caused by the pull of the moon's gravity on the Earth.

What's all this, then?

Gravity!

c. 145 BC Clever thinking

Hipparchus from Nicaea, in present-day Turkey, used geometry to figure out how far away the moon was from the Earth. His calculations gave an answer of 403,623 km (250,800 miles) — which is very close to what scientists believe today.

Moon   Sun

Earth

So, if I equate these and divide that...

c. 1065　Shapeshifter

The Chinese thinker, Shen Kuo, realized the moon was a sphere. He explained its different shapes, which we call phases. As it orbits the Earth, the amount of the moon that is lit by the Sun changes:

 1. New Moon 　 2. Waxing Crescent 　 3. First Quarter

4. Waxing Gibbous 　 5. Full Moon 　 6. Waning Gibbous

7. Last Quarter 　 8. Waning Crescent 　 9. New Moon

17th and 18th centuries　I spy with my little eye...

Many early astronomers used telescopes to study the moon. They called its mountains *"terrae"*, which means lands in Latin. The valleys looked like large lakes, so they were called *maria*, meaning seas.

That's the Sea of Tranquility.

In fact, there's little or no water on the moon. Modern scientists think the *maria* are made of hard lava from prehistoric, now extinct, moon volcanoes.

1969　Humans on the moon

Finally, in 1969, after all that gazing and dreaming, the USA *Apollo 11* mission landed on the moon. Pictures were sent back to Earth as Neil Armstrong became the first person to step on the moon. More trips to the moon were made during the 1970s. Several countries are planning new moon missions this century.

1610
Genius Galileo

Would you look at that?!

Around 1610, Galileo adapted a new battle invention, a telescope, into a tool for sky gazing (see pages 16-19). He saw that the spots on the surface of the moon were valleys and the paler areas were mountains. He also discovered that even though the moon orbits the Earth, the same side always faces us.

1959　The dark side

In 1959, the unmanned Soviet *Luna* missions entered space. Some landed on the moon and others orbited it. They brought back photos of the unseen, dark side of the moon.

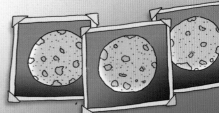

One small step for man, one giant leap for mankind!

Neil Armstrong, the first person to walk on the moon.

25

Archimedes was said to be so excited by his discovery, he leaped out of the bath and ran naked through the streets.

Eureka!

In the 3rd century BC, an ancient Greek inventor named Archimedes got into his bath. On seeing the water sploshing over the sides, he is said to have shouted "Eureka!" – "I've found it!" But what exactly had he found?

What is density?

The density of a substance means how much matter it contains for its size. For example, one cubic cm of gold weighs 19.3 grams. It contains more matter, and has greater density, than one cubic cm of silver, which weighs 10.5 grams.

$1cm^3$ of gold

$1cm^3$ of silver

They are both the same size, but the gold is heavier because it is denser – more densely packed with matter.

Hiero's crown would probably have been made in the shape of a wreath of leaves, making its volume hard to work out.

Bathtime brainwave

According to legend, King Hiero II of Syracuse had asked Archimedes for help. Hiero had paid a goldsmith to make him a golden crown. But, when it arrived, Hiero suspected the man had cheated by mixing cheaper silver with the gold and keeping some of the gold for himself.

To find out if this was true, Archimedes needed to know the density of the crown. Silver is less dense than gold, so knowing the density of the crown would tell him if some silver had been mixed in. To measure density, you need to know an object's weight and volume. It was easy to measure the crown's weight, but its volume was a puzzle, as it was such a complicated shape.

When Archimedes got into the full bath, some water flowed over the sides. He suddenly saw that you could measure the volume of any object by dropping it into water, and measuring how much of the water was pushed upwards. He calculated the crown's density, and found that the goldsmith was indeed a cheat.

Did it really happen?

This story is very famous, but we don't know if it's true. It was first written down by a Roman writer, Vitruvius, 200 years later – so it could be made up. But Archimedes did make important discoveries about water and density...

Why things float

In the "Eureka" story, Archimedes saw that when you put an object into water, some of the water gets displaced, or pushed out of the way. And it's true that Archimedes did observe this carefully. He saw that whether or not an object floats depends on its density, and how much water it displaces. Objects float because water pushes them up. The water pushes up with the same force as the weight of the water displaced by the object. Less dense objects weigh less than the water they displace, so they float.

Archimedes definitely discovered this, as he explained it all in his own book, *On Floating Bodies*.

Archimedes designed a huge ship for King Hiero II, the *Syracusia*. A ship floats because its shape – a curved hull filled with air – gives it a very low total density.

Eureka moments

Many scientists claim to have had "Eureka" moments. Big ideas and discoveries often seem to happen like this, when the brain suddenly sees things in a new way. In 2003, scientists scanned people's brains while they were doing puzzles, and saw a part of the brain sparking whenever they suddenly cracked a problem.

If an object displaces water that weighs as much as itself, it floats.

If an object cannot displace water that weighs as much as itself, it sinks.

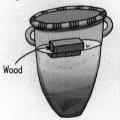

Wood

Stone

A block of wood is less dense than water. Because it is light for its size, it easily displaces its own weight in water.

A block of stone is much denser than water. It cannot displace enough water to match its own weight, so it sinks.

Archimedes' screw
As you turn the screw, its thread spirals upward and lifts water with it.

Archimedes showed that the longer a lever is, the more pushing force it can create. He said:

Give me a place to stand, and I will move the Earth!

More discoveries

Archimedes was one of the greatest thinkers ever. He came up with dozens of discoveries and inventions. He invented the Archimedes' screw – a kind of pump for lifting water – and built an early planetarium, a model of the night sky. He also discovered how levers work (see opposite).

Ouch!!
Hmmmm...

Newton and the apple

It's a famous old story. One day in 1666, Isaac Newton was in his garden when an apple fell on his head. Suddenly, he realized what had made it fall. He had discovered gravity! In fact, of course, it didn't happen quite like this...

Brilliant brain

Newton studied different scientific topics – including physics, mathematics, optics (the study of light) and astronomy – especially the work of Copernicus and Galileo (see page 20). Newton could apply his brilliant brain to many different kinds of problems and find amazing new ways of seeing and understanding them.

As well as studying all these subjects, he became a Member of Parliament. He was also made Master of the Mint, meaning he was in charge of making England's new coins.

Home for the holidays

Isaac Newton had been studying maths, physics and astronomy at Cambridge University. In 1665, the university was forced to close because of a deadly disease called the Plague, so Newton went home, to Lincolnshire, and spent his time thinking about scientific problems.

Newton later reported that he had seen an apple falling in the garden, and that this made him think about gravity. Of course, he wasn't the first to notice the pull of gravity. Everyone knew that objects fell to the ground. But Newton wondered how this pulling force worked, and how far away from the Earth it reached. Could it stretch as far as the moon, or beyond?

Gravity, planets and orbits

Newton came up with a new theory about gravity. He suggested that it wasn't just a pulling force from the Earth. He realized that all objects pull other objects towards them. The more massive an object is, the stronger its gravitational pull.

This explains why the moon circles the Earth, and the Earth circles the Sun. Their forward movement means they should fly off into space, but the pull of gravity between them holds them in orbit.

Newton saw how gravity made objects orbit each other in space.

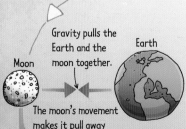

Gravity pulls the Earth and the moon together.

Earth

Moon

The moon's movement makes it pull away from the Earth.

The two forces are in balance, so the moon circles the Earth.

A book of ideas

Later, Newton returned to work at Cambridge. Over the years, he developed many new scientific ideas. The astronomer Edmond Halley asked him to write them down in a book, and offered to pay to have it published. So, in 1687, Newton's book *Philosophiae Naturalis Principia Mathematica* appeared. Now known as the *Principia*, it is one of the most important books in the history of science.

Bad temper

Newton was famous for being very bad-tempered, rude and difficult to be around. He was often so busy thinking about his work that he would ignore people, wander off and go back to his desk. He had many furious arguments with scientific colleagues, including Robert Hooke (see page 60).

Three laws of motion

Besides Newton's important mathematical discoveries and ideas on gravity, the *Principia* stated three laws of motion:

1. An object will keep still or keep moving unless a force acts on it to change this.

2. The more massive an object is, the more force is needed to make it speed up or slow down.

3. To every action, there is an equal and opposite reaction. (So, if you push an object, you feel it pushing back at you.)

When you push toy cars, they obey Newton's laws of motion.

Changing the world

Newton's work was hugely important – because before him nobody had really understood gravity, or the ways forces pushed and pulled at objects.

In the 1900s, Einstein and others found that Newton's theories don't always apply (see page 36). But scientists and engineers today still rely on his laws to predict how objects will move and behave.

Rocket scientists use Newton's laws to plan the route of a rocket through space.

On course for the moon!

Zoom!

Yikes!

CRASSHHH!

Electricity

Electricity has totally transformed our lives. Imagine having no TV, no computer, no electric lights, mobile phones or email. Of course, no one invented electricity – it's always existed in nature. But it took scientists centuries before they found out how to use it.

Lightning is a kind of electrical spark caused by static electricity collecting in thunderclouds. Some early societies thought it was a sign that their gods were angry.

Electric amber

If you rub a plastic comb on something made of wool, you give the comb a slight static electric "charge" that can attract small things, such as bits of paper. The ancient Greeks knew about this. Thales, who lived around 600 BC, described how a lump of amber, if rubbed on cat fur, could pull tiny objects towards it and make sparks.

In the 1500s, people began to study this again – including Queen Elizabeth I's doctor, William Gilbert. He found he could make other substances, such as jet (a type of stone) and glass, do the same thing. In 1600, Gilbert used the term *electricus* – from *elektron*, the Greek word for amber – to describe what was happening.

Static or current?

When an electrical charge collects in an object, it's called static (that is, "still") electricity. Sometimes, a build-up of static electricity can result in a spark leaping to another object. This is what causes lightning, and the shocks you can get from supermarket trolleys.

When electricity flows along a wire or through a substance, it's known as an electric current.

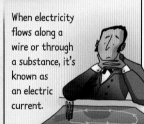

A shock in a jar

It's electric!

In the early 1700s, inventors came up with several devices for creating electric charge. But they couldn't keep or control the electricity. Then, in 1745, Pieter van Musschenbroek invented something called a Leyden jar, which can keep an electric charge stored in it.

In 1746, physicist Jean Antoine Nollet demonstrated a Leyden jar to the king of France. He released the store of electricity in the jar into a circle of royal guards. They all got a shock!

Franklin's foolhardy feat

In 1752, a great US writer and inventor named Benjamin Franklin carried out an experiment to show that lightning was made of electricity. He flew a kite in a storm, with a key on the end of the kite string. Electricity from the clouds flowed down the wet string and through the key. Franklin found he could get a spark to jump from the key.

Don't try this yourself. The kite experiment was incredibly dangerous, and several people died trying to repeat it. But he did find out a lot about how electricity can flow through materials that conduct or carry it.

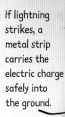

Franklin invented the lightning conductor to protect buildings from lightning strikes.

If lightning strikes, a metal strip carries the electric charge safely into the ground.

Jumping frogs' legs

In the 1780s, Italian biologist Luigi Galvani found that applying electric charge to dead frogs' legs could make them twitch. One day, though, a frog's leg jumped by itself when he hadn't used electricity. He had simply touched it with a knife.

Galvani thought the leg must contain its own electricity supply. But his colleague Alessandro Volta disagreed. He thought electricity had flowed because two different metals — the knife and the metal tray the leg was on — had come into contact through the wet frog muscle.

Electric legs

You might still be wondering why electricity made the frogs' legs jump.

In fact, as Galvani discovered, living things do use electricity in their bodies. The brain and the nerves use electrical signals to send messages around the body. When electricity flowed into the frog's leg muscle — even after it was dead — it gave the muscle a signal that made it move.

The first battery

Volta experimented with using two metals to make electricity. In 1800, he built a stack of zinc discs, silver discs and pieces of cardboard soaked in salt water. When he connected the top and the bottom of the pile with wire, electricity flowed through it! This "Voltaic pile" was the first battery. In a modern, 'dry' battery, a chemical reaction between two metal compounds creates a flow of electricity.

An early version of Volta's Voltaic pile

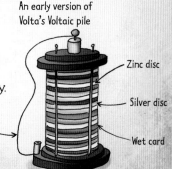

Zinc disc

Silver disc

Wires

Wet card

Feeling the heat

Everyone knows what heat feels like. But do you know what heat actually is, and how it works? This perplexing puzzle took many great thinkers several centuries to solve.

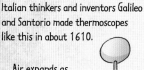

Italian thinkers and inventors Galileo and Santorio made thermoscopes like this in about 1610.

Air expands as it heats up.

Water level drops.

The first thermometers

People have known for a long time that when air, water and other substances get hotter, they expand, or take up more space. Around 1600, inventors used this knowledge to make the first simple thermometers, or thermoscopes. They used expanding air to make the water level in a tube move up and down, showing changes in temperature.

The first true thermometer, with a scale, was made by an Italian doctor, Santorio Santorio, in about 1612. In 1641, Grand Duke Ferdinand of Tuscany made a thermometer from a sealed glass tube, with a liquid (alcohol) inside. And in 1664, English experimenter Robert Hooke used the freezing point of water as the starting point on his thermometer's temperature scale.

In the 1700s, Daniel Fahrenheit invented a mercury thermometer and a temperature scale, named after him. Swedish astronomer Anders Celsius created the Celsius scale, with 100 degrees between freezing and boiling.

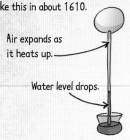

The Grand Duke of Tuscany's 1641 thermometer was the first to use an expanding liquid, rather than air, in a sealed tube.

Sealed tube

Vacuum (empty space) inside

Alcohol expands as it warms up.

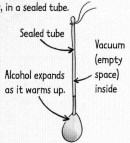

In 1724, German engineer Daniel Fahrenheit made the first thermometer containing mercury, a liquid metal. He also invented a temperature scale – Fahrenheit (F).

212°F = boiling point of water

98°F = human body temperature

32°F = freezing point of water

But what is heat?

But still nobody knew what heat really was. Many people thought it was caused by an actual substance, called "the caloric". This mysterious fluid was thought to flow from hot things into less hot things – which explained why hot objects warm up the colder things around them.

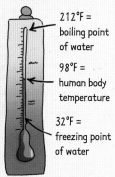

The temperature on a very hot, sunny day measures around 30-40°C (Celsius). That's 86-104°F.

32

Heat is energy!

In some ways, the caloric theory didn't make much sense. In 1798, US-born inventor Benjamin Thompson described how, when he drilled a hole in a metal cannon, the cannon got so hot that it could boil water. But before the experiment, the drill, the cannon and the water were all cold. Thompson saw that heat had not "flowed" from anything hot. Instead, it had been created by friction – the movement of the drill grinding against the metal.

A few decades later, in the 1840s, English physicist James Prescott Joule agreed with Thompson. He showed that a paddle turning in water warmed up the water, and that electricity running through a wire made the wire hotter.

Heat, Joule said, was just a form of energy – like motion, electricity, sound and so on. One form of energy could turn into another – although the total amount of energy stayed the same. For example:

Friction (caused by rubbing things together) turns movement energy into heat energy.

Burning wood or coal turns chemical energy stored in the fuel into heat energy.

Moving molecules

So what happens to substances when they heat up? A new idea, the kinetic theory, replaced the "caloric". In 1734, Daniel Bernoulli had said that gas pressure was caused by the particles in a gas zooming around and hitting the walls of their container. Scientists knew that heat makes gas expand, increasing its pressure. So heat must actually be making the molecules move faster and hit harder. In the 1860s, Scottish scientist James Clerk Maxwell used experiments to show that the kinetic theory did make sense – and we still use it today.

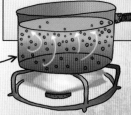

When you heat water in a pan, the molecules in the pan pass on their energy to the molecules in the water.

Thompson used this experiment to show that friction can boil water.

He cut a section from a cannon and put it in a tank of water. As he drilled into the piece of metal, the water got warmer and finally boiled.

The kinetic theory

The kinetic theory says that as a substance gets hotter, its molecules move faster. In fact, this explains why things change between solid, liquid and gas. As the molecules move faster, they break apart from each other more easily.

As a solid heats up, it eventually melts and becomes a flowing liquid.

And as a liquid heats up, the molecules eventually escape into the air and become a gas.

Heat flows between substances that are touching each other because their molecules bump against each other.

Help! We're all doomed!

Oooh, look what the compass did!

Electromagnetism

Long ago, sailors in stormy seas noticed that when lightning struck nearby, their compass needles would turn, as if pulled by a magnet. In fact, electricity (which lightning is made of) and magnetism are closely related.

But what is electromagnetism?

Electricity and magnetism are caused by something called charge. The tiny particles that make up atoms can have a positive (+) or a negative (-) charge. Positively charged and negatively charged particles pull towards each other.

But what makes this happen, and how can the pulling force reach out across empty space? The truth is, scientists still aren't really sure. There are many puzzles about the universe that we haven't yet solved (see page 88).

This diagram shows the different types of electromagnetic energy in the Electromagnetic Spectrum. The difference between them is that the electromagnetic waves have different lengths. The shorter the wavelength, the more energy the waves carry.

Making the link

In the early 1800s, current (flowing) electricity was a new discovery. Several thinkers had wondered if it was related to magnets, but this was hard to prove. Then, in 1820, Danish physicist Hans Christian Ørsted found that if he put a compass close to a wire with electricity running through it, the magnetic compass needle moved. Where there was an electric currrent, there was a magnetic force, too.

Faraday's fields

News of Ørsted's results spread, and other people tried out more experiments with electricity and magnets.

In 1821, English physicist Michael Faraday made a needle circle around a magnet by running an electric current through them. Later, in 1831, he found that the same process worked in reverse. He could create an electric current by moving a magnet through a coil of wire.

Faraday suggested that electricity and magnets both had "fields" – areas of force reaching out around an electric wire or a magnet. These fields influenced each other – a moving electric field created a magnetic field, and vice versa.

short wavelength

Gamma rays have very short electromagnetic waves – shorter than an atom is wide. They are harmful to living things.

X-rays have a short wavelength. They can pass through some substances, but not others.

Ultraviolet (UV) light is short-wave light. We can't see it, but UV light from the Sun can damage our skin.

The light we can see is made of electromagnetic radiation too. The different colours are caused by slightly different wavelengths.

Maxwell's mathematics

After Faraday died in 1867, Scottish mathematician James Clerk Maxwell began to study electric and magnetic fields. He discovered mathematical rules for how they behaved and influenced each other. In fact, he found that they were so closely related, one never existed without the other – they could be seen as a single force. The word "electromagnetic" was used to describe this type of energy.

Albert Einstein (1879-1955)

James Clerk Maxwell (1831-1879)

Isaac Newton (1642-1727)

James Clerk Maxwell isn't very famous today, but many scientists think he was just as important as great discoverers like Newton and Einstein.

Electromagnetic waves

In the 1860s, Faraday had wondered if "vibrations" in the electric and magnetic fields could spread out through space. Maxwell found that this was true. Electromagnetic energy could travel in the form of vibrations, or waves, that disturbed the electromagnetic field – just as a wave moving across the sea disturbs the water.

Maxwell called this electromagnetic radiation. When he calculated how fast it moved, he found it was the same as the speed of light. He saw that light was a type of electromagnetic wave – and that there must be others, too.

Space travel
Electromagnetic waves can travel through air, and through materials such as wood and glass. But they can also travel across empty space, where there is nothing for them to move through. Because of this, we can use radio to contact astronauts in space, and radio telescopes to detect electromagnetic radiation given off by distant objects in space.

Calling Ground Control, over!

The electromagnetic spectrum

Maxwell died in 1879, aged just 48. Soon afterwards, other scientists did discover new kinds of electromagnetic radiation, with waves of different lengths, such as radio waves and X-rays. The full range of electromagnetic radiation is known as the Electromagnetic Spectrum.

long wavelength

Infrared radiation is long-wave light. It is given off by hot objects, and we feel it as heat. We can't see it, but we have cameras that can.

Microwaves are a type of radio wave. They might sound small, but they are quite long electromagnetic waves.

Radio waves are very long electromagnetic waves – each wave can be several kilometres long. We use them to carry signals and messages long distances.

Einstein in 1951, when he was 72

In later life, when he was very famous, Einstein was a scruffy figure with wild white hair. The popular image of a "mad scientist" is largely based on him.

Einstein

German-born genius Albert Einstein is one of the best-known, yet least-understood, scientists of all time. His brilliant mind found amazing new ways to understand the universe. But they're hard to get your head around!

Growing up

Famously, Einstein did poorly at school. But as a boy in the 1880s, he was very interested in science. His father and uncle were electricians, and he was amazed by electricity. When his father gave him a compass, that fascinated him too. How did magnetism make the needle point North?

Aged 23, Einstein started work at a patent office (where inventions are registered) in Bern, Switzerland. It was a lowly job, but it gave him time to think about the scientific questions that puzzled him. They were huge questions about the nature of electromagnetism, time, space, energy and matter (the "stuff" that things are made of). His aim was to find a set of rules that linked all these things together.

Light and electromagnetism

Einstein talked about light and its speed, but he could just as well have been talking about any electromagnetic wave (see page 35). Light is a kind of electromagnetic energy, like radio waves, gamma rays or X-rays. All electromagnetic waves travel at the same, constant speed, which Einstein named "c".

The speed of light

In 1687, Isaac Newton had set out his laws of motion (see page 29) on the basis that time flowed steadily, and space was fixed. Time and space did not bend, stretch or change.

But Einstein disagreed. Other scientists had shown that the speed of light didn't change, even if it came from a moving light source. Einstein decided that it was the speed of light that was fixed, or constant, and gave it a name – "c". According to his calculations, this meant that time, space and matter were *not* fixed – they were all "relative" to one another.

Einstein wondered what would happen if you could ride a light wave, and travel at the speed of light. He thought that however fast you went, light would never seem to stand still.

Relativity

Einstein revealed his ideas to the world in several papers published in 1905. They included his *Special Theory of Relativity*. It says that there is no such thing as one fixed place, point, or time in the universe. Instead, we can only measure things in relation to other things, and things change relative to each other. For example, Einstein said that if one object is moving very fast relative to another, time will pass at different rates for the two objects.

That sounds ridiculous, and people laughed at Einstein because he hadn't done any experiments to prove it. But when other scientists did, they found he was right.

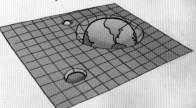

One illustration of the *Special Theory of Relativity* imagines two twins. One stays on Earth while the other zooms around space at almost the speed of light. When they meet again, the astronaut twin will be younger, as time has gone by more slowly for him.

$E=mc^2$

Einstein also saw that energy and matter are different forms of the same thing, and can be changed into each other. His famous equation $E=mc^2$ is about this. It means that the energy (E) in matter is equal to the amount of matter (m), multiplied by the speed of light (c) squared (squared means multiplied by itself).

This means that even a small amount of matter can be converted into a huge amount of energy, if its atoms are split apart. This knowledge led to the development of the atom bomb, which Einstein regretted (see page 49).

But I don't get it!

Don't worry. Einstein's ideas are hard to understand, even for other scientists. That's partly because these theories don't have much to do with everyday life. In fact, although Einstein proved Newton wrong, Newton's laws do still make more sense for most everyday measurements. Einstein's theories are important, but they are only important for very extreme situations.

Aargh! It's too hard!

The problem of gravity

In 1916, Einstein published a new theory, *General Relativity*, to try to explain gravity. He saw space and time as one thing – spacetime. He said that heavy objects such as planets made spacetime curve, so that other objects fell towards them. Today, this is still one of several explanations for gravity.

You can imagine Einstein's theory of gravity by seeing spacetime as as a giant stretchy sheet with heavy planets on it. The planets make dents in the sheet, which other objects roll into.

What is light?

Even though light is all around us, scholars have argued over what it is, how it travels and why it behaves the way it does.

2,500 years ago
Greek ideas

Ancient Greek philosophers had many different ideas about light. One of them, Empedocles, thought the goddess Aphrodite placed a flame inside each person's eye which enabled them to see.

Another philosopher, Ptolemy, believed that rays of light shone from the eyes, letting things in the rays' path be seen.

Euclid was more scientific – he studied perspective and was the first person to suggest that light moved in straight lines.

c. 1000   Alhazen

A great Arab scholar, Ibn al-Haytham, or Alhazen, investigated how light behaved. He suggested that objects reflect light (from a source such as the Sun) in rays, and that when these rays enter the eye they allow us to see. He imagined each ray as a stream of tiny particles of light moving very quickly.

1672   Splitting light

Among his other discoveries, Isaac Newton (see page 28) did lots of experiments with light. The most famous one involved shining light through a crystal called a prism. This made the light split into seven colours. He passed the beam through a second prism, and they shone as a single white beam again.

Another English experimenter, Robert Hooke, thought that light might move in waves. But Newton didn't believe this, because waves move around obstacles (such as islands in the sea), and light doesn't. Instead, like Alhazen, he said light was made up of extremely tiny pieces of matter.

light

prism spectrum

point of ligh

Light moves in waves...

1690   Making waves

A Dutch physicist Christiaan Huygens had other ideas. He developed a new, detailed wave theory for light. He said that light moved in waves in straight lines, and that different light waves heading in different directions or paths might interfere with each other.

c. 1800 Brilliant beams

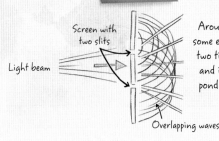

Screen with two slits

Light beam

Overlapping waves

Around 1800, a British thinker, Thomas Young, conducted some experiments based on Huygens's theory. In one, he used two tiny slits to create two beams of light. They fanned out and interfered with each other, like two sets of ripples on a pond, forming a pattern on a screen. This proved that light could behave in the same way as water waves.

1840s - 1880s Many hands make light work!

Visible light

Electric field

Magnetic field

During the 19th century lots of scientists investigated light. In 1847, Michael Faraday noticed that a beam of light could be affected by a magnetic field. In 1888, a German scientist, Heinrich Hertz, studied radio waves and compared them to light. These experiments and many others established that visible light is part of something scientists call the Electromagnetic Spectrum – a range of energy waves of different lengths (see page 34).

1905 Einstein and photons

Although the wave theory explained most of the ways that light behaves, there were a few things that still puzzled scientists. In 1905, Albert Einstein solved some of these problems by suggesting that light had both wave and particle properties. Sometimes it behaves as a wave, and sometimes as if it's made of little particles of matter. These wave-particles are called photons, and can be imagined as tiny "packets" of energy. But scientists today are still debating exactly how light works.

wave

wave-particles

photon

electron

energy

metal

$E = Mc^2$

1926 Speed of light

Many scientists, such as Galileo (in 1638) and a Danish physicist, Ole Rømer (in 1676), tried to measure the speed of light. Some thought it moved so quickly that its speed would never be known. It wasn't until the 19th and 20th centuries that clocks became accurate enough to test it. Two French physicists, Hippolyte Fizeau (in 1849) and Léon Foucault (in 1862), came up with fairly accurate measurements. But the answer wasn't settled until the 1920s.

Light

Rotating mirror

Mirror

In 1926, a US physicist, A. A. Michelson, measured the time taken for light to travel from one mountaintop to another and back again. From this, he calculated that the speed of light is approximately 300,000 km (186,411 miles) per second – which was the right answer.

From alchemy to chemistry

Chemistry is the science of how substances behave, join together and break apart. It helps people to make all kinds of things we use every day, such as medicines, washing powder and shampoo. But did you know that modern chemistry grew out of a mystical world of secret codes and magic spells, which was known as alchemy?

What is alchemy?

People have been doing things like heating up rocks to get useful metals out of them for more than 5,000 years.

But long ago, nobody understood how things like this worked. If a precious metal such as gold could come from stones, they reasoned, maybe you could make it out of anything. These ideas led to the practice of alchemy. Alchemists experimented with all kinds of substances to try to make something valuable.

The philosopher's stone

Alchemists spent many years searching for, or trying to create, a magical substance called the philosopher's stone. They believed it could turn other metals, such as lead, into gold just by touching them. Many also thought that the philosopher's stone could give a person eternal youth or make them live forever. Despite many efforts, no one ever seems to have found it...

Like the ancient Greeks, most alchemists believed everything was made up of just four basic elements: Earth, Air, Fire and Water.

Earth   Air   Fire   Water

Alchemists used code-like symbols to stand for the four elements and many other substances too.

We now know that a lot of alchemy was nonsense, but some alchemists were very clever. The great physicist Isaac Newton, for example, was a keen alchemist.

Many alchemists wanted to make gold out of cheaper "base" metals.

Others hoped to create a magic medicine called the Elixir of Life, which could cure all illnesses.

Alchemy was like chemistry, but less scientific. Instead of carefully studying the facts, many alchemists thought that things like magic spells, secret signs or the position of the stars could help them. And a lot of them were cheats, who made fake gold and drugs to sell. Over time, though, some alchemists' experiments led to useful inventions, such as inks, porcelain and effective medicines. This practical, non-magical side of alchemy became known as "chymistry".

To mix, heat and process their chemicals, alchemists invented many types of equipment that are still used in chemistry labs today.

Arabian alchemy

The word alchemy comes from *al-kimiya*, which means the "transmutation" or "changing" of things in Arabic.

Arab alchemists were among the first to do proper carefully recorded experiments. One of the most famous was Abu Musa Jabir ibn Hayyan, also known as "Geber", who lived around the year 800. He found out how to make many useful chemicals, such as hydrochloric acid, and invented better ways of making steel and glass. He also said: "The first essential in chemistry is that you must perform practical work and conduct experiments."

Boyle's *Skeptical Chymist*

One of the most famous chemists was Irish-born Robert Boyle. He discovered several gases, and saw that there must be many different elements. In 1661, he wrote a book, *The Skeptical Chymist*, which argued that the mystical, magical aspects of alchemy were nonsense. Like Geber, Boyle said "chymists" should test ideas with experiments, and use a clear, simple system for naming chemicals.

The origins of modern chemistry

A hundred years later, French chemist Antoine Lavoisier followed these ideas and changed the way chemistry was done (see box), paving the way for modern chemistry. These changes are often called "the chemical revolution".

Lavoisier's revolution

Lavoisier set up new ways of doing chemistry experiments and measurements.

He discovered and listed many new chemicals and elements (see page 45).

He used experiments to find out what really happens when things burn.

Oxygen... hydrogen... sulphuric acid...

He came up with a naming system for chemicals that is still used today.

He declared that chemical reactions can change substances, but not create or destroy matter.

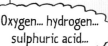

Lavoisier even helped to invent the metric measuring system.

Metric measuring flasks are a common sight in today's chemistry labs.

> I give this spirit, unknown hitherto, the new name of "gas".

Jan Baptist
van Helmont

Discovering gases

People used to think that air was a single, pure substance, one of only four basic elements. But air isn't pure — it's a mixture of gases. And there are many other gases besides. Not surprisingly though, as most gases are invisible, they weren't the easiest things to discover and study.

What is gas?

In the 1640s, Belgian alchemist Jan Baptist van Helmont found that when he burned charcoal, much of it changed into an invisible substance he called "wild spirit" — a gas which escaped into the air. He saw that coal mines, fermenting grapes and living things gave off similar gases.

He noted that most gases are invisible, and can't be held in an open container. He even invented the word "gas", from the Greek word "chaos" (as gases have no fixed shape).

Squashing and bumping

In 1662, Irish experimenter Robert Boyle tried squashing air to compress it, or make it take up less space. He found that doubling the pressure on a mass of air always compresses it to half its previous size. This rule applies to all gases, and is known as Boyle's Law.

In 1734, Daniel Bernoulli, a Swiss mathematician, said that a gas creates its own outward pressure, as the tiny particles in it bounce around and bump against the walls of the container. Boyle and Bernoulli were starting to understand how gases worked, but they hadn't found many individual gases. But that was all about to change...

Catching gases

Around 1730, English inventor and experimenter Stephen Hales developed a brilliant device for catching gases, now known as the pneumatic trough. It made working with gases, testing them and discovering new gases much easier for other chemists.

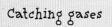

Gas being released

Gas being collected

Trough

In a pneumatic trough, gas bubbles up through water and is trapped at the top of an upturned glass jar.

Robert Boyle used a simple J-shaped tube like this to carry out experiments with compressed air.

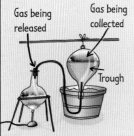

Adding more mercury makes the pressure on the air greater.

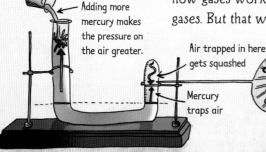

Air trapped in here gets squashed

Mercury traps air

The particles in a gas shoot around in all directions, hitting the walls of the container and creating an outwards pressure - but the pressure of the mercury is greater, so the volume of the gas is still reduced.

Joseph Black

Gas escaping

Lump of lime

When Black heated the chalk, it gave off a gas, leaving behind lime.

Fixed air

Next on the scene was a Scottish chemist, Joseph Black. In around 1753, he tried heating up calcium carbonate – also known as limestone, or chalk. This released a kind of gas, leaving behind a substance called lime. The gas and lime could then be combined to make chalk again.

Black named the gas "fixed air" (as it could be "fixed" into a solid substance). He also tried leaving some lime in the open air, and it gradually turned back into chalk. From this, Black saw that natural air must contain some "fixed air" – which we now call carbon dioxide. We now know that carbon dioxide makes up about 0.5% of the air.

Chalk

He then mixed the lime with the gas, and found they joined back together to make chalk again.

Lighter than air

For many years, alchemists had known that when metals dissolve in acid, an invisible substance often formed, which burned easily. In 1766, English chemist Henry Cavendish collected and studied this gas. As well as being very flammable (it caught fire easily) he found it was 14 times lighter than air. He had discovered hydrogen.

Fizzy drinks
During his experiments with gases, Joseph Priestley found that he could dissolve carbon dioxide in water. It made the water fizzy and bubbly, with a sharp, tangy taste. Soon, Priestley's invention, soda water, was being sold as a drink, with things added to change the taste.

Oxygen

English clergyman and chemist Joseph Priestley discovered several different gases. The most important was oxygen, which he released in 1774 by heating up "calx" – a chemical made of oxygen and mercury. The great French chemist Antoine Lavoisier (see page 41) gave oxygen, hydrogen and many other gases their modern names.

Since then, chemists have discovered many more gases, with hundreds of uses in the modern world.

Natural gas, mainly made of methane – which is a gas emitted by cows – is widely used as a fuel.

Helium gas is used to fill party balloons.

Some cars can run on hydrogen gas.

Snort! ...
Giggle...

What?

Later Greeks called Democritus "the laughing philosopher". According to stories about him, he found everything funny.

How small?

Atoms are really, really small. They're so tiny that it's hard to imagine just how many there are. One page in this book is about a million atoms thick. One small raindrop contains around 50 million million million atoms.

I can't see them...

When Boyle tried compressing air, he could feel it bouncing back at him – like a spring.

The air hath a spring!

Atoms and elements

Since ancient Greek times, people have wondered exactly what things are made of. Why are there so many different materials? And if we could look really closely at matter, what would we see?

Ancient atom ideas

Some ancient Greeks said that although things looked different, everything was basically the same. It was all really made of water, for example – or air – just in different forms. But, other Greeks said there were four elements, or types of things: earth, air, fire and water.

Two thinkers who lived around 400BC, Democritus and his teacher, Leucippus, had another idea. They said all matter was made of tiny particles, or atoms. There were many different types of atoms, arranged in different patterns to make different materials. For centuries, though, nobody believed them and continued to think that everything was made up of the four basic ingredients.

Atoms in the air

It was nearly 2,000 years later, in the 1650s, that Robert Boyle experimented with compressing (squashing) air. Since air could be compressed, he said, it must be made of lots of tiny particles, spaced far apart, with gaps in between. Things like water and metal must contain more of them, as they were harder to squash.

Boyle also thought Aristotle was wrong about the four elements. Instead, he said that there were many "simple bodies" – basic substances that couldn't be broken down into simpler parts.

44

Finding the basics

Alchemists and chemists soon began trying to find all the different types of "simple bodies" (now called chemical elements). They used chemical reactions to find out which substances could not be broken down any further. They kept finding more and more of them – such as gold, mercury and oxygen. And they realized that elements like these could join together to make more complex materials, known as compounds.

Dalton sums it up

It was a British teacher named John Dalton who finally put all these ideas together. In 1803, he perfected his "atomic theory". Like Democritus and Leucippus, he said that each element was made of its own, unique type of atom.

Air is not an element... but a mixture of several gases.

French chemist Antoine Lavoisier played a big role in the search for the elements. He published a list of 33 of them in 1789.

Dalton said each different type of atom had a different amount of mass (the amount of matter in it).

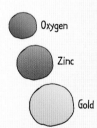

Oxygen

Zinc

Gold

Atoms could join other atoms to make molecules. And so elements could form compounds. Oxygen and hydrogen are elements.

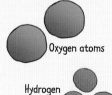

Oxygen atoms

Hydrogen atoms

Water is a compound. A water molecule is made of two hydrogen atoms and one oxygen atom.

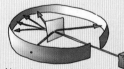

Although he was right, Dalton couldn't actually see atoms. He calculated all this from the weights and proportions of the elements in different compounds. Scientists can now see atoms using powerful electron microscopes, and scientists have identified over 100 elements.

What's inside?

No one knew what atoms were like inside until 1909, when New Zealand-born scientist Ernest Rutherford came up with this experiment:

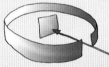

Tiny particles were fired at a very thin sheet of gold leaf.

Most shot straight through, but some bounced off.

Rutherford saw that an atom must have a solid centre, or nucleus, surrounded by mostly empty space. Most of the particles shot through the space, but a few hit a nucleus.

Tiny particles called electrons whizz around the nucleus.

Nucleus

Empty space

Roentgen made this X-ray image of his wife Bertha's hand.

X-rays are a type of high-energy electromagnetic wave. The X-rays were used in very strong doses and sometimes made people ill.

Radioactivity

Some scientists have given their lives for their discoveries. One of the most famous of all was Marie Curie, who devoted years to studying radioactive materials – before anyone realized how dangerous they were.

How radioactivity works

Radioactive elements such as uranium release energy from the nucleuses of their atoms. The nucleus gradually breaks down over time, giving off energy called radiation. Depending on the element, the radiation can take the form of waves called gamma rays, or tiny particles called alpha and beta particles.

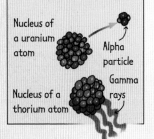

Nucleus of a uranium atom

Alpha particle

Gamma rays

Nucleus of a thorium atom

Becquerel wrapped a photographic plate in black paper to keep light out, and put the crystals on top.

Sunlight made the crystals glow, and they made an image on the plate. Becquerel thought they must be giving out X-rays.

But then he found that even when they were in a dark room, and didn't glow, the crystals still made a photographic image. So he realized they must be giving out some other kind of energy.

Mysterious rays

In 1895, Wilhelm Roentgen, a German physics professor, detected strange rays coming from a cathode ray tube (a vacuum tube with an electric current running through it). He named them X-rays. They could pass through soft substances and make an image on a photographic plate. This was very useful for looking inside the human body – and X-rays are still used for this today.

Curious crystals

Other scientists were fascinated by X-rays and tried out all kinds of tests with them. In 1896, French physicist Henri Becquerel set up an experiment to see if fluorescent (glowing) materials gave out X-rays as well as light. He used potassium uranyl sulphate – fluorescent crystals that glow after being in strong sunlight.

The crystals didn't need any extra energy (such as electricity or sunlight) to make them give out energy. They formed an image on a photographic plate even in a darkened room. So this strange form of energy came from the crystals themselves. What Becquerel had discovered was radioactivity. It would be left to two other great scientists, Marie and Pierre Curie, to understand it.

Radioactivity revealed!

Polish-born Marie Curie and her French husband Pierre Curie were Becquerel's colleagues at the University of Paris. In the late 1890s they studied his crystals, and found that the mysterious energy was coming from one of the elements in them — uranium.

They tested other substances too, and found other radioactive elements. They invented the name "radioactivity" for this type of energy, and worked out ways to measure exactly how radioactive different elements were.

The Curies used an ionization chamber like this. Radioactive substances made electricity flow through the air in the chamber. The strength of the current showed the amount of radiation.

Among other substances, the Curies tested pitchblende, the ore that uranium comes from.

They found it was much more radioactive than uranium alone. In it, they discovered two more radioactive elements: polonium and radium.

Pierre Curie died in a road accident in 1906, but Marie Curie took over his job as a professor, and carried on their work. She and other scientists found that radioactive elements give off less and less radiation over time. The time it takes for the radiation level to drop by half is known as its half-life.

Nobel family

In 1903, Pierre and Marie Curie and Henri Becquerel were jointly awarded the Nobel Prize in Physics for their discovery of radioactivity.

Eight years later, in 1911, Marie Curie won the Nobel Prize in Chemistry for her work on radium and polonium — the first ever double Nobel winner. The Curies' daughter Irène Joliot-Curie also won a Nobel Prize in 1935 for work on radioactivity.

A Nobel Prize medal

For good and bad

Since it was discovered, scientists have found many valuable uses for radioactivity, such as calculating the age of rocks (see page 11). But they have also discovered that radioactive waves and particles damage our bodies, and can cause illnesses such as cancer. Marie Curie died in 1934 from a disease called aplastic anaemia, probably caused by all the radioactive elements she had handled.

Medical tools and supplies are cleaned, or sterilized, using a powerful beam of radiation to kill all germs.

It's ancient!

Radiometric dating measures radioactivity to find out how old rocks and fossils are.

Inside atoms

Only a hundred years after the discovery that everything is made of atoms, people learned that atoms are *not* the smallest things that exist. So, what's inside an atom?

Atomic building blocks

In 1917, Ernest Rutherford proved that one kind of element, hydrogen, has the most basic of all atoms: a nucleus made up of a single particle he called a proton, with a single electron whizzing around it. All other elements are made up of multiple protons in the nucleus, surrounded by a matching number of electrons.

But something didn't add up. The nucleus of most atoms appeared to be too heavy to be made up *only* of protons. The missing particles, named neutrons, were discovered in 1932 by English physicist James Chadwick.

Splitting the atom

Chadwick's discovery unleashed a new field: nuclear physics. During the 1930s, two German chemists, Otto Hahn and Lise Meitner, devised experiments to bombard the nucleus of uranium atoms with neutrons.

Hungarian-born Leó Szilárd designed machines called particle accelerators that can force particles to whizz around at fantastic speeds. Soon, chemists used these machines to conduct Hahn's experiments, and found that high-speed neutrons can break atoms apart, creating new elements – and unleashing new, smaller particles.

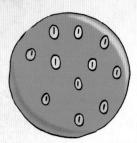

In 1904, the most up-to-date diagram of an atom was known as the "plum pudding model". It showed a blob dotted with little electrically charged 'raisins'.

By 1912, Ernest Rutherford radically re-drew the diagram (see page 45). His version had a small, central blob called a nucleus. The 'raisins', now known as electrons, whizzed around near the edge.

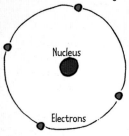

Nucleus

Electrons

Danish physicist Niels Bohr developed Rutherford's model by suggesting that electrons whizz around the nucleus in set pathways, known today as *orbitals*.

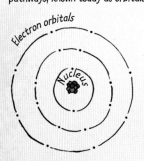

Electron orbitals

Nucleus

Chemists today still use the Bohr model as a teaching tool, although it doesn't truly represent reality.

Krypton nucleus

Uranium nucleus

Loose neutron

Unknown particles

Neutron

Boron nucleus

The particle zoo

During the 1950s and 60s, teams around the world built bigger and better particle accelerators. Experiments revealed all sorts of new particles inside atoms — so many that some described the results as a "particle zoo".

> Had I foreseen this, I would have gone into botany.

Wolfgang Pauli,
Austrian particle physicist

Atoms turned out to be a combination of six different electron-sized particles called *quarks*, held together by energy bundles called *gluons*.

Also in the mix were incredibly tiny particles called *neutrinos*, found in many varieties. Even worse, every particle had its own almost-invisible opposite, called an anti-particle!

In 1899, German physicist Max Planck was desperate to understand how atoms behaved. He put forward a radical theory: energy is not always a continuous wave. Instead, it exists in little packets he called "quanta".

The study of how tiny particles, such as electrons, quarks and neutrinos behave, is known as *quantum mechanics*.

Standard model

Since the 1970s, most physicists have followed a theory of particles known as the Standard Model.

According to the model, there are two fundamental types of particles, *fermions* and *bosons*.

If subatomic particles were a sandwich, fermions would be the slices of bread, and bosons would be the butter that allows the slices to stick together.

Recreating the Big Bang

The biggest-ever particle research facility, known as CERN, was set up in 1954 by a cross-European team of scientists. It is currently home to six separate particle accelerators, including the Large Hadron Collider (LHC). This is so powerful that when switched on, it almost recreates the intense heat and pressure of the very first second of the Big Bang.

CERN particle physics laboratory

In 2012, detectors in the LHC found evidence of one of the most elusive particles yet — the Higgs boson.

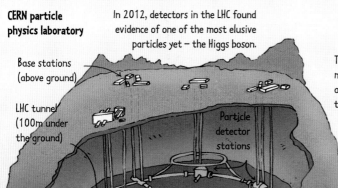

Base stations (above ground)

LHC tunnel (100m under the ground)

Particle detector stations

The Higgs boson is very heavy (for a minute particle) but only exists for an instant. It enables other particles to have different masses.

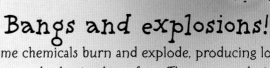

Bangs and explosions!

Some chemicals burn and explode, producing loud bangs and releasing lots of gas. These are explosives, and can be used in fireworks and weapons.

9th century "Black powder"

In the 9th century, Chinese alchemists were trying to create a potion that would give everlasting life. Instead, what they got when they mixed together saltpetre, sulphur and charcoal was a dark powder that burned and exploded. In the following centuries, this "black powder", or gunpowder, was used to make bombs and ammunition for cannons and guns.

10th century Fireworks

Fireworks were originally used in Chinese ceremonies to pray for happiness and to scare away evil spirits. Black powder and other chemicals were fired into the sky to create fantastic explosive displays.

1627 Digging and mining

Black powder was first used to blast rock in Europe in 1627 at silver mines in Slovakia.

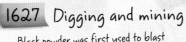

1807 Explosive experiments

In 1807, an English chemist, Humphry Davy, isolated a new element by running an electrical current through caustic soda. The element he found was pure sodium metal. It has to be stored in oil, because it reacts quickly with any moisture in the air and blows up.

Danger!

1846 Nitroglycerine

In 1846, an Italian chemist, Ascanio Sobrero, discovered nitroglycerine. This extremely explosive liquid was more powerful than black powder. It was very unstable, though, and caused accidental explosions — so it was banned in many countries for years.

Ooops!

1866 & 1875
Dynamite and gelignite

In 1866, a Swedish scientist, Alfred Nobel, combined nitroglycerine with a stable solid to make a safer explosive called dynamite, for use in mining and building. A more powerful jelly-like version, gelignite, was developed in 1875.

1930s Plastic explosives

In the 1930s, army scientists and engineers combined plastics with explosive materials to produce soft explosives. These could be moulded like plasticine and were easier to transport. They're often used to demolish buildings.

1940s Bigger bombs

Atomic weapons were developed in the USA during the Second World War. A group of famous scientists, including J. R. Oppenheimer, Enrico Fermi and Albert Einstein, realized that splitting apart the nucleus of an atom would cause a powerful explosion.

An atomic bomb contains explosive material and radioactive chemicals. When the explosive is blown up, the nuclear chemicals begin a powerful chain reaction. Then, as the atomic nucleuses break apart, a huge and destructive radioactive explosion occurs.

The first atomic explosion was named the Trinity test, it took place in the desert of New Mexico, USA in July 1945.

1980s
Exploding pillows

During the 1980s, car manufacturers developed a positive use for an explosion — an airbag. In a car crash, a sensor detects any sudden stop and allows two chemicals to react together and produce a large volume of nitrogen gas. The gas inflates the bag and provides a cushion to protect the driver or passenger from injury.

20th century On the scent

Dogs have very sensitive noses and can be taught to hunt for explosives by scent. Honeybees can be trained to associate the smell of explosives with sugar. Computer programs can track the swarm and use it to detect suspicious packages.

Follow me!

This 20,000 year-old "Ishango bone" was discovered in central Africa in 1960.

Bones scratched with marks like this were probably used for counting days and months.

Measuring time

We can't stop time, or control it. We don't even really know what it is. But for thousands of years, we've been finding ever more accurate ways to measure it as it whizzes by.

The Sun and the Moon

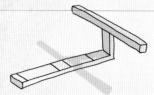

This Egyptian shadow clock casts a shadow on a stick marked with time divisions. As the Sun climbs higher, the shadow gets shorter.

The most obvious signs of time passing are natural cycles – the rising and setting of the Sun each day, and the phases of the moon from new to full and back again.

Ancient people took note of these patterns to make the first calendars. As early as 5,500 years ago, the ancient Egyptians had a calendar similar to ours. It had 12 months of 30 days each, and the days were divided into hours and minutes. An extra five days were added at the end of the last month to make up the 365 days in a full year.

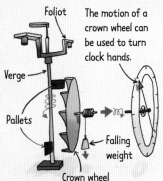

Foliot

Verge

Pallets

The motion of a crown wheel can be used to turn clock hands.

Falling weight

Crown wheel

Medieval clocks used a "verge and foliot escapement" like this. A falling weight on a string pulled a wheel around. As the wheel turned, its teeth caught on two tabs, called pallets, creating a regular clicking action.

In about 1500, German locksmith Peter Henlein invented spring-driven mechanical clocks. As there was no dangling weight, he could make small, portable watches too.

Shadow clocks

The Sumerians, ancient Egyptians and other early peoples used shadows to help them work out what time it was. A stick in a fixed position cast a moving shadow through the day, as the Sun moved across the sky.

Time machines

The ancient Greeks, Romans and Chinese were building early mechanical clocks around 2,000 years ago. They used water dripping through a hole to drive wheels and cogs that rang bells or showed the time on a dial. Later, in medieval Europe, new types of clocks were invented that used falling weights or wound-up springs to make the parts move – but they didn't keep time very well.

The pendulum: natural time

In about 1600, the great Italian thinker Galileo (see page 21) studied the science of a weight on a string, called a pendulum. He claimed that, given a certain length, a pendulum always takes the same amount of time to swing to and fro. He saw that pendulums were useful for measuring time, because they had a natural rhythm, not an artificial mechanism.

Galileo didn't build a pendulum clock himself, but Dutch astronomer Christiaan Huygens did in 1656. Pendulum clocks were the most accurate clocks invented so far.

A playground swing is a kind of pendulum. Whether you swing just a little or right up high, the swing doesn't change its rhythm (unless you push with your feet). Try it!

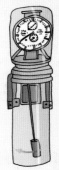

By 1889, this German-built "Reifler clock" was so accurate it lost only 1/100 of a second per day.

20th-century time

Pendulum clocks were good, but there are far tinier, more reliable rhythms in nature, that can be used to make mindbogglingly accurate clocks.

In the 1880s, French scientist Pierre Curie (see page 46) and his brother Jacques found that an electric current makes some minerals, such as quartz, vibrate very quickly. The vibrations can be used to drive a clock. The first quartz clock was made in 1927.

Then, in the 1940s, scientists began using even faster vibrations – the natural vibrations of atoms – to time clocks. Atomic clocks are the most accurate clocks of all.

Extra seconds
The spinning of the Earth is gradually slowing down, so each day is very slightly longer than the day before. This means the official length of a second gradually becomes too short. So every year or two, the official, internationally agreed time has to be adjusted to add an extra second or "leap second".

And the time is...

Today, people around the world use International Atomic Time, a standard time based on an atomic clock driven by the vibrations of a caesium atom. In 1967, one second was officially defined as 9,192,631,770 caesium

Come on! Keep up!

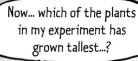

Now... which of the plants in my experiment has grown tallest...?

Scientists often find facts out by counting and measuring things.

The story of numbers

Numbers and counting are part of most people's everyday lives. They're also essential to science, which involves lots of measuring, comparing and calculating. But we didn't always have the numbers we have today.

No numbers!

There are some languages still in use today that have no numbers in them at all. The Pirahã people from South America, for example, don't see a need to count things, so they don't have words for numbers. Instead they have one word for "a bit" and another for "lots".

How many did you catch?

A bit!

Keeping a tally

The first evidence of counting – notches marked on sticks, stones and bones – dates from over 30,000 years ago. This basic kind of counting is called "tallying". You simply use one mark for each item you want to count. So if you are counting 20 people, you make 20 marks. Sometimes, the marks are grouped together in bunches, like this:

Counting on our fingers

Fingers were probably the first counting tools. People today count in base 10 – using multiples of 10, such as 10, 100, 1,000 and so on – probably because we have 10 fingers. The ancient Egyptians were the first people to develop this system, as early as 6,000 years ago.

The ancient Egyptian number system
The Egyptians used different symbols for the numbers 1-9, 10, 100, 1,000 and so on.

1 2 3 4 5 6 7 8 9

10   100   1,000

They showed larger numbers by combining the symbols for the different groups:

1 x 1,000   2 x 100   3 x 10   5

Counting in 60s

But other peoples used a different system. About 1,000 years later, the Babylonians, who lived in what is now Iraq, were using a base 60 number system. So, instead of counting in groups of 10, they counted in groups of 60. This system probaby died out because it was hard to use.

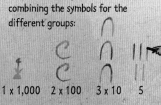

= 1,235

A place for zero

The ancient Egyptians had different symbols for 1s, 10s, 100s and so on, but no symbol for 0 (zero). So if they wanted to write the number 207, they wrote it like this:

2 x 100 ⟶   ⟵ 7

There was no need for a zero to show "no 10s".

The Romans were the same. They used letters for numbers, and didn't use zero. So 207 looked like this:

CCVII

2 x 100   5   2 x 1

In fact, most ancient counting systems didn't use the number zero. But, from about 400BC, people in ancient India had other ideas. They used base 10 too, but instead of symbols, there were just 10 numbers – 1, 2, 3, 4, 5, 6, 7, 8, 9, and 0. You used single numbers to count up to 9. After that, you used 1 again – but moved it left one place, and added a 0, to make 10. In this system, the position of the numbers shows what they stand for. Zero is used as a "place holder" to fill in empty spaces.

10

One group of 10   No 1s

207

Two 100s   No 10s   Seven 1s

Modern numbers

As you can see all around you, the Indian number system and its symbols – now called "Arabic numerals" – were the ones that eventually spread across the world. It lets us write big numbers easily, using just a few symbols,

The ancient Greeks thought about the idea of a number "nothing", but they weren't sure it was really a proper number.

Counting in 2s

You could use any number as a base number – if we wanted, we could count in groups of 5, 14 or 199. It's just that we're used to using 10. Computers use a base 2, or "binary", number system, like this:

1 = 1
2 = 10 (one 2, and no 1s)
3 = 11 (one 2, and one 1)
4 = 100 (one 4, no 2s and no 1s)

...and so on. This means that computers can do all their calculations using just two symbols, 0 and 1. These can be represented by switching electrical current off and on inside the computer.

...011010001
11010100
0010100
101011...

If you were still using the ancient Egyptian or Babylonian system to write down numbers, your maths books would be huge!

Puzzling primes

Since ancient times, people have noticed that some numbers can't be divided by other numbers. These "prime numbers" still puzzle mathematicians to this day.

The ancient Greeks saw that some numbers naturally broke down into groups, while prime numbers didn't. For example, 12 isn't a prime number, but 13 is.

12 stones can be arranged in three rows of four, or two rows of six.

13 stones can only be arranged in a single line, not matching rows.

Prime definition

A prime number is a number that can only be divided by two numbers: itself and 1. People used to think 1 was a prime number, but it can only be divided by one number – 1 – so it is now not counted as a prime. Below you can see all the prime numbers between 1 and 100.

2	3	5	7	11	13	17
19	23	29	31	37	41	43
47	53	59	61	67	71	73
79	83	89	97			

The ancient Greeks

Pythagoras, an ancient Greek thinker, and his followers were very interested in the mysterious properties of numbers. Around 400 BC, one of Pythagoras's followers, Philolaus, said that some numbers were composite (that is, they could be composed, or made up, of smaller numbers) – while prime or "incomposite" numbers could not.

A Greek mathematician named Euclid also studied prime numbers. He showed that however high you count, you will always find new prime numbers (though they occur less often the higher you go). In other words, there are an infinite number of primes. He also found that non-prime numbers can be broken down into different combinations of prime numbers multiplied together.

Not long after that, around 200 BC, another Greek thinker, Eratosthenes, invented a grid for calculating prime numbers, known as "the sieve of Eratosthenes".

Prime time again

After the Greeks, no one found out much more about prime numbers for centuries. Then, in the 1500s and 1600s, people began to look at them again. French lawyer Pierre de Fermat was fascinated by primes and came up with several theories about how to calculate them. But, some mathematicians found his theories weren't completely right. There didn't seem to be any totally reliable formula for finding prime numbers.

Although Fermat didn't find a perfect way to predict primes, he did find out a lot about them. One type of prime number, Fermat Primes, is named after him.

Pierre de Fermat

I have found a very great number of exceedingly beautiful theorems!

Working it out

So, over the years, mathematicians spent long hours doing divisions of bigger and bigger numbers, to see if they were primes. By 1600, Italian mathematician Pietro Cataldi had found two six-figure primes, 131,071 and 524,287. In 1876, Édouard Lucas, a Frenchman, showed that 170141183460469231731687303715884105727 was a prime number. It was the biggest prime ever discovered using hand-written calculations.

Édouard Lucas

Computer calculations

In the 1940s and 1950s, computers developed to the point where they could be used to calculate new prime numbers. This made the job much, much faster — although testing really big numbers still takes computers a long time. We have now found prime numbers that are millions of digits long. They're so big that writing just one of them down would fill 50 books the size of this one!

What's the point of primes?

For a long time, prime numbers had no practical use. Scientists only studied them in the hope of finding meaningful patterns. They still haven't had much success.

But, computer scientists have now found an important use for primes. If you have a large non-prime number, it's very hard to find out which prime numbers can be multiplied together to make it. This secret knowledge can be used for putting information into code to send between computers. Only a computer that knows the

Periodical cicadas

Prime numbers appear in nature too. Periodical cicadas (a type of insect) spend most of their lives as larvae (young) underground. Every 13 or 17 years (depending on the species), they reach adulthood, emerge above ground, mate and lay eggs. 13 and 17 are both primes. A prime-number life cycle helps the cicadas to avoid being hunted by animals with shorter life cycles, such as 2 or 3 years. It means they won't usually meet many adult predators, giving them a better chance of survival.

We often use codes to send sensitive or secret information between different computers.

57

Mathematical curiosities

Ever since humans began counting and calculating, they've come across all kinds of curious and interesting number puzzles and magical-seeming patterns and shapes.

c. 2,800 BC

Magic squares

According to ancient Chinese legend, when the River Lo flooded, the people prayed to the river god to save them. A turtle appeared from the water, with a strange inscription on his back.

The marks said to be on the turtle were a type of magic square. They could be written like this:

4	9	2
3	5	7
8	1	6

Add up any row of three numbers – horizontally, vertically or diagonally – and you always get the same number (in this case, 15).

Magic squares have appeared in many cultures since ancient times. Modern mathematicians have designed much bigger, more complex versions.

c. 2000 BC The story of pi

What do you get if you divide the circumference (length around the edge) of a circle by the diameter (the length across the middle)?

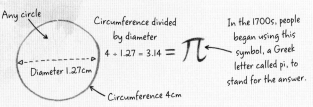

Any circle

Diameter 1.27cm

Circumference 4cm

Circumference divided by diameter
$4 ÷ 1.27 = 3.14 = \pi$

In the 1700s, people began using this symbol, a Greek letter called pi, to stand for the answer.

Pi is roughly 3.14. Magically, it's the same for all circles, however big they are.

The ancient Egyptians and Sumerians both knew a bit about pi over 4,000 years ago. Then, in about 250 BC, Greek thinker Archimedes calculated pi as 3.1419. And around the year 490 a Chinese scholar, Zu Chongzhi, reached a more accurate figure of about 3.14159265. Using computers, we've been able to calculate pi to millions of decimal places. But we'll never get it exactly right, as the decimal numbers in pi keep going on forever...

c. 550 BC Pythagoras's triangle

The life of the ancient Greek philosopher Pythagoras is surrounded in mystery. He lived in the 500s BC, and had a group of followers who passed on his knowledge. He is most famous for Pythagoras's theorem, all about right-angled triangles.

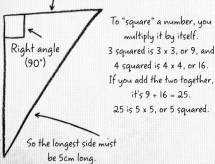

This side measures 3cm. 3 x 3 = 9.

The theorem says that in a right-angled triangle like this, the two shorter sides "squared" always add up to the longest side squared.

Right angle (90°)

This side measures 4cm.
4 x 4 = 16.

So the longest side must be 5cm long.

To "square" a number, you multiply it by itself.
3 squared is 3 x 3, or 9, and 4 squared is 4 x 4, or 16. If you add the two together, it's 9 + 16 = 25.
25 is 5 x 5, or 5 squared.

c. 400 BC Infinity

Ancient Indian mathematicians wrote about infinity – a name for an endless amount that we can never count. However big a number is, you could always add 1 to it. So numbers are infinite – they go on for ever...

This is the symbol for infinity. It was first used by English mathematician John Wallis in the 1650s.

c.300 BC The golden ratio

Are some rectangles better than others? The ancient Greeks thought so. They found that if a rectangle was about 1.61 times longer than it is wide, it had a special property.

It's mean and extreme!

Length 1.61 units

Width 1 unit

Greeks such as Euclid called this the "mean and extreme" ratio. It later became known as the golden ratio, or golden mean.

If you mark off one end of the rectangle to make a square...

...you will be left with a smaller rectangle with exactly the same shape as the first.

The Greeks thought that a rectangle with this ratio must be magical and perfect, so they often used it in buildings. It was also popular in the Renaissance, from about 1450 to 1700, and you can still see it in many buildings and paintings today.

1858 A Möbius strip

Amazingly, two German mathematicians, August Ferdinand Möbius and Johann Benedict Listing, both discovered the Möbius strip separately, in 1858. You can see what they discovered by making a Möbius strip for yourself – it's easy:

1. Cut a narrow strip of paper, about 30cm (12 inches) long by 3cm wide (1¼ inch).

2. Bring the strip around to make a loop, then flip one end over so that the strip is twisted. Then tape or glue the ends together.

Your Möbius strip has some amazing properties. If you draw a continuous line along it, you'll find you've drawn on both sides. In fact, a Möbius strip only really has one side!

Now cut carefully along the middle of the strip to divide it in two. You can't! You just end up with a bigger loop. Weird!

1202 Fibonacci numbers

In about 1202, an Italian mathematician known as Fibonacci worked out a number sequence to show how the population of rabbits might increase if they were left to breed. The sequence looked like this:

1 1 2 3 5 8 13 21...

Can you see how it works? At each step, you add together the previous two numbers to make the next. In fact, Fibonacci wasn't the first to find this pattern – ancient Indian people had discovered it too. Later mathematicians found that it was closely connected to the golden ratio, and often occurs in nature.

If you draw a rectangle using two adjacent Fibonacci numbers for the sides, you end up with the golden ratio! A series of these rectangles can make a spiral...

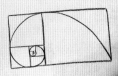

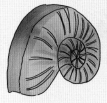

...and spirals the same shape are often found in nature, for example in seashells.

1920 A googol

As the number of numbers is infinite, there are some pretty big numbers. One of these is a googol. It is a 1 followed by 100 zeroes. A googol is so big, it's bigger than the number of atoms in the whole universe.

A googol was invented in 1920, when US mathematician Edward Kasner asked his nine-year-old nephew Milton Sirotta to think up a name for a big number. Milton also invented an even bigger number, a googolplex – 1 with a googol zeroes after it!

Classifying creatures

What do you call a small, furry, purring pet animal? The domestic cat has hundreds of names and nicknames in many languages. But scientists everywhere know it by a scientific Latin name, *Felis catus*. Sorting living things into groups and giving them scientific names is called classification, and it dates from ancient times.

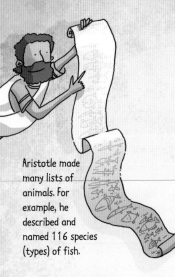

Aristotle made many lists of animals. For example, he described and named 116 species (types) of fish.

Aristotle and Theophrastus

Ancient Greek writer and thinker Aristotle developed an early classification system around 330 BC. For example, he divided animals into those with blood and those without, and according to whether they walked on land, flew in the air or swam in water. His student, Theophrastus, wrote two books on plants, dividing them into groups according to where they grew, their size and what they were used for.

A new system

Aristotle and Theophrastus had made a great start, but their categories didn't always make much sense. For example, sardines, turtles and whales all swim in the sea. But they breathe, feed and reproduce (have babies) in completely different ways.

In the 1500s, 1600s and 1700s, people began exploring more and more of the world, and zoologists and botanists discovered thousands of previously unknown species (types) of living things. They couldn't all fit into the old system, so people came up with new ways of classifying living creatures. The biggest and most important system was invented by a Swedish naturalist named Carl Linnaeus — and a version of it is still used today.

Linnaeus's life

The family of Carl Linnaeus (see below) hoped he would be a priest, like his father. But he was so passionate about plants they let him study science and medicine instead.

The family was poor, but Linnaeus's enthusiasm impressed many wealthy friends, who paid for him to study. Linnaeus loved writing long lists of living things and getting all the details exactly right.

Apple tree –
Malus domestica

Carl Linnaeus

Common daisy –
Bellis perennis

Grass snake –
Natrix natrix

Linnaeus's "System of Nature"

Carl Linnaeus was born in Sweden in 1707, and worked as a doctor and as a teacher of botany (plant science). He was fascinated with plants and discovered many species himself, but explorers also sent him samples of plants and animals they had collected from around the world.

By the end of Linnaeus's life, his book *Systema Naturae*, or *The System of Nature*, had grown to over 3,000 pages long.

Throughout his life, Linnaeus worked on a new way of classifying living things. His method divided plants and animals into groups, then split each group into smaller groups, and so on. Instead of sorting them according to where they lived or their uses to humans, Linnaeus looked at their shapes and how they lived and reproduced.

He wrote his system down in his book *The System of Nature*. It was first published in 1735, but he revised it many times. By 1770, it listed over 12,000 living things.

New names

Before Linnaeus, living things did have scientific names, but they were long-winded Latin descriptions that could fill several lines. Linnaeus invented the "binomial" system, in which each creature had a simple two-part Latin name.

The word "binomial" simply means "two names" in Latin.

The first name shows the family. The second name shows the species.

Felis catus

Miaow!

Latin names are always written in italics, and the first word starts with a capital letter.

Levels of life

Linnaeus used five main levels in his System of Nature. For example, the pet cat is:

Kingdom: *Animalia* (animals)
Class: *Mammalia* (mammals)
Order: *Carnivora* (carnivores)
Genus: *Felidae* (cats)
Species: *Felis catus*

Today we use a more complex division system with seven levels. A classification of the pet cat looks like this:

Kingdom: *Animalia* (animals)
Phylum: *Chordata* (having a spinal cord)
Class: *Mammalia* (mammals)
Order: *Carnivora* (carnivores)
Genus: *Felidae* (cats)
Family: *Felis* (small cats)
Species: *Felis catus*

After Linnaeus

Since the 1700s, scientists have discovered millions more living things, and made several changes to Linnaeus's system. But many of the plant and animal groups he named are still used, as well as his binomial method.

Megamouth sharks were discovered as recently as 1976. It was given the scientific name *Megachasma pelagios*.

Hello, I'm new to science...

There are creatures in my mouth! They're alive!

Antonie van Leeuwenhoek was the first person to see single-celled bacteria in tooth plaque.

We're all made of cells!

All living things are made of tiny living units called cells. They are so small, we can't even see them. So how did we find out about them?

Seeing more

In the 1600s, there was a great leap forward in many areas of science thanks to the invention of microscopes and telescopes.

For centuries, people had used curved lenses to make things look bigger. But around 1600, better glass-making and lens-grinding methods led to much better, stronger lenses. People also learned to combine two or more lenses for more powerful magnification.

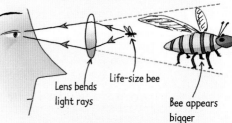

A lens is a curved piece of glass. It makes objects look bigger by bending the rays of light that come from them.

Lens bends light rays

Life-size bee

Bee appears bigger

Microscope types

The first microscopes were invented in the early 1600s. There were two main types – compound and single-lens.

In a compound microscope, two or more lenses were arranged in a row. The great Italian inventor and thinker Galileo made an early version in 1609. Robert Hooke used a compound microscope that could magnify about 30x (that is, make things look 30 times bigger).

Hooke's microscope

The single-lens microscope had just one lens. Van Leeuwenhoek made his own, very powerful single-lens microscopes. He melted glass to make tiny spherical lenses that could magnify up to 300x.

Lens

A van Leeuwenhoek microscope

Hooke's cells

Robert Hooke was a great English experimenter. In the 1660s, while working for the Royal Society (an official group of scientists) in London, he used a compound microscope to study objects from nature. In 1665, he published *Micrographia*, a book of amazing drawings of tiny things including pictures of moss under the microscope, in which plant cells were clearly visible. Hooke came up with the name "cells" to describe the tiny compartments he saw in a piece of cork. They reminded him of the cells (tiny rooms) that monks lived in.

Hooke's drawing of cork under the microscope showed the plant cells looking like little rooms. Cork comes from the bark of a type of oak tree.

Teeny creepy-crawlies

Hooke's work inspired many others to look more closely at living things. One was Antonie van Leeuwenhoek, a Dutch fabric trader. Van Leeuwenhoek was brilliant at making microscope lenses, which he used to check his fabrics closely. But after reading Hooke's *Micrographia*, he decided to study the natural world too.

During the 1670s, van Leeuwenhoek discovered tiny tiny things, such as algae, living in drinking water. He also studied tooth plaque, and saw single-celled living creatures, which we now know as bacteria. In 1676 he wrote to the Royal Society about these "animalcules" or tiny animals. The members of the Royal Society were so amazed, they thought van Leeuwenhoek must be crazy. But by 1680, they realized he was right. He also described individual human body cells, such as red blood cells.

Bacteria in tooth plaque

Microscopic creatures found on a beach

Van Leeuwenhoek made detailed drawings of the tiny creatures he saw through his microscopes.

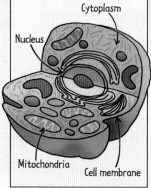

Inside a cell

Over time, scientists saw cells in more and more detail. They found that each cell has its own headquarters, or nucleus, and many other parts. This diagram shows some of the main parts of an animal cell:

Cytoplasm

Nucleus

Mitochondria

Cell membrane

What cells do

Hooke and van Leeuwenhoek had definitely discovered cells, but what were they for? As better and better microscopes were made, people could look at cells more closely, and saw they were the building blocks of all living things. In the 1830s, Czech cell expert Jan Purkyne found many different types of cells in the human body. And in the 1840s, scientists saw thread-like structures, which were later named chromosomes, inside cells.

Around 1880, German scientist Walter Flemming studied the way cells split in two to make new cells, making copies of their chromosomes as they did so. He named this process mitosis. But, what were chromosomes for, and how did the cells know what to do? Find out more on page 68.

In mitosis, a cell divides in two to make two new "daughter" cells. This is how living things make new cells so that they can grow and repair themselves.

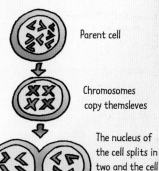

Parent cell

Chromosomes copy themsleves

The nucleus of the cell splits in two and the cell starts to divide.

Two new "daughter" cells form.

How plants grow

When you sow seeds in the soil, plants grow. One acorn can grow into a giant oak tree, weighing many tonnes. But unlike humans and animals, plants don't eat. So where do they get the food they need to grow bigger and bigger?

Soil food

Ancient Greek thinker Aristotle pondered the question of what plants eat. He saw that plants didn't have stomachs. So he thought they must use the Earth as a kind of stomach, using their roots to suck up all the food and water they needed from the soil.

Do plants live on soil?

Around 1640, Belgian experimenter Jan Baptist van Helmont did an experiment to test Aristotle's theory (see left). He filled a large pot with soil, and planted a tiny willow tree in it. After five years, the tree weighed as much as a full-grown man, but the soil hadn't disappeared. It was almost exactly the same. From this, van Helmont saw that plants did not "eat" soil. So he decided they must build their leaves, branches and stems mainly from water.

Van Helmont was right that plants need water. A tree is about 50% water. But what about the rest?

Life on Earth

The Earth looks very green from space, because of its billions of plants.

If it weren't for plants, we wouldn't exist, and nor would most other life on Earth. Photosynthesis lets plants turn the Sun's energy into a different form of energy – the chemicals stored in plant matter. Animals get energy by eating these plants – or by eating other animals that feed on plants. Plants also keep us all alive by soaking up carbon dioxide gas, and giving out oxygen gas, which animals need to breathe.

Plants and air

Around 1720, English naturalist Stephen Hales carried out lots more plant experiments. He grew plants inside sealed chambers, and measured the air and water levels around them. From this he discovered that plant leaves took in gases from the air, and gave out water, and suggested that leaves might soak up light too. He was right, but how did it work?

Another English experimenter, Joseph Priestley, wanted to find out how plants changed the air around them. In 1771 and 1772, he did these two famous experiments:

I found that the air would neither extinguish a candle nor inconvenience a mouse!

Joseph Priestley

Priestley burned a candle in a sealed jar until it went out and wouldn't relight.

But after he grew a plant in the same jar for a few weeks, the candle was relit and burned again.

Priestley also found that a mouse could breathe for longer in a sealed jar if there was a plant in the jar too.

The candle flame and the mouse both needed a particular gas (later named *oxygen* by Lavoisier) – so Priestley concluded it must be coming from the plants.

At this time, oxygen and other gases in the air were only just being discovered, by Priestley and other chemists. Over the next few years, they discovered that plant leaves took in the gas carbon dioxide, and gave out oxygen.

Light is the key

In 1779, Dutch botanist Jan Ingenhousz tried testing plants in light and dark conditions. He showed that plants did take in carbon dioxide and give out oxygen – but only in sunlight. They needed light for the process to work.

In 1845 a German scientist, Julius Robert von Mayer, finally put all these elements together. He studied energy, and how it changed from one form to another. He saw that plants must take their energy from sunlight, using it to make the chemicals they needed to grow their leaves and other parts. This process is now called photosynthesis. Plant leaves take in sunlight, water and carbon dioxide. These react together to make water, oxygen and food chemicals.

A new name

In the 1800s, scientists used the name "assimilation" for the way plants used sunlight to make food. But the same word was also used to describe changes in animals' bodies. In 1893, US plant scientist Charles Reid Barnes decided the plant process needed its own name. He came up with two options:

Photosyntax! ...and... Photosynthesis!

...which both mean, roughly, "building with light" in Greek. "Photosynthesis" was the one that became widely used.

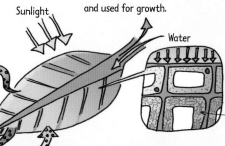

Food made in the leaf is carried around the plant and used for growth.

Sunlight

Oxygen

Water

Photosynthesis actually happens in microscopic parts called chloroplasts, found inside plant cells.

Water   Carbon dioxide

BZZZZZZZZZZZ!

The story of evolution

Meganeura dragonflies lived up to 300 million years ago. They looked like dragonflies today – but measured 70cm (28 inches) across!

200 million years ago, dinosaurs, pterodactyls and giant dragonflies lived on the Earth – and there were no birds, snakes or humans. We know about life in the past from fossils (see page 82). But why have living things changed?

Fossil finds

In the early 1800s, the great French fossil expert Georges Cuvier studied thousands of fossil remains. He found that animals from the past often resembled modern animals.

For example, the woolly mammoth was similar to the modern elephant, but not the same. Cuvier also saw that many prehistoric animals had died out, or become extinct.

Yikes!

Dinosaur disaster

Cuvier said that extinct animals must have been wiped out by natural disasters, such as floods. Scientists now think this is partly true. Dinosaurs probably died out because of volcanic eruptions or an asteroid hitting the Earth.

Stretchy necks

Cuvier thought that although living species could die out, they could not change. But other naturalists wondered if species could "evolve", or change gradually, over time.

Cuvier's colleague Jean-Baptiste Lamarck, thought that animals might change during their lives, and then pass on these changes to their babies. One famous example suggests that giraffes might have got their long necks by stretching them to reach for food.

Lamarck was not quite right about this. As scientists now know, if a plant or animal changes during its lifetime, this change will not be passed onto its babies. For example, if you lose a leg in an accident, your children won't be born with one leg. But Lamarck took a big step by thinking about how evolution might work.

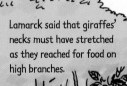

Lamarck said that giraffes' necks must have stretched as they reached for food on high branches.

Lamarck thought that a giraffe with a longer neck would then have babies with long necks. He believed that, over time, this would have made giraffes' necks longer and longer.

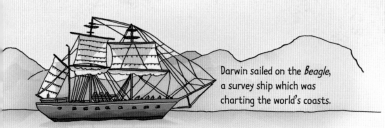
Darwin sailed on the *Beagle*, a survey ship which was charting the world's coasts.

1. Some giraffes have slightly longer necks than others. As their food grows on trees, giraffes with longer necks can reach more food.

2. The best-fed giraffes tend to live longer and have more babies. They pass on their body shape to their young.

Voyage of a lifetime

In 1831, a young Englishman, Charles Darwin, set out on a five-year trip as a ship's naturalist. He was only 22 and not a scientist, but he was passionately interested in nature. On the journey, he collected many fossils and samples of living things, and made piles of notes and sketches.

After he returned in 1836, Darwin studied his findings and came up with a new theory of evolution. He called it "natural selection". It showed that species could change over time, because of slight differences between members of the same species. Darwin's idea of how giraffes got their long necks is shown on the right.

3. Over the generations, longer-necked giraffes do better, and the species changes. Eventually, all giraffes have very long necks.

Great minds think alike

At first, Darwin kept his theory quiet. He knew it could upset many Christians, who believed all species had been created in a perfect, final state just after the creation of the Earth.

But in 1858, another naturalist, Alfred Russel Wallace, wrote to Darwin with the very same ideas. Darwin saw that it was time to make his theory public. A year later, in 1859, he published a book, *On the Origin of Species*, explaining natural selection.

As he had expected, it caused an uproar. Many church leaders were furious. But some others, as well as a lot of scientists, supported Darwin. Since then, more and more fossil evidence, as well as the discovery of genes and DNA (see page 68), has backed up the theory of natural selection.

Some Christians were angry when Darwin suggested that humans could have evolved, instead of being specially created by God. They mocked him by comparing him to an ape.

"Survival of the fittest"

Darwin often used the phrase "the survival of the fittest" to describe natural selection. But "fittest" didn't mean healthiest or strongest. It meant most fit, or most suitable. The creatures that fit their surroundings best were the ones that survived best, and so were "selected" by nature to pass on their qualities to the next generation. This explains how living things have adapted to suit their habitats so well.

Prrrrrrrrr...

When a mother and father tiger have babies, the babies are always tiger cubs. That seems obvious – but until the 20th century, no one knew how it worked.

Genes and DNA

By 1900, scientists knew that living things were made of cells. But they didn't yet know how cells do their jobs. How do cells know how to build our bodies, and pass this information on from one generation to the next? What makes an orange an orange and not a lemon, and why do some people have blue eyes and some brown?

Mendel's garden peas

In the 1850s, an Austrian-born monk named Gregor Mendel found part of the answer by studying pea plants. He bred tall pea ones with short ones and sowed the seeds. What grew were not medium-sized plants, but tall ones only.

Mendel decided the cells in the seeds must contain something he called a "factor", that made them grow to be either tall or short. The "tallness factor" didn't combine with the "shortness factor" – it overrode it.

Mendel bred tall pea plants together – and found that some some of them produced small plants.

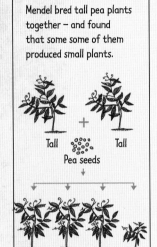

Tall   +   Tall

Pea seeds

Tall   Tall   Tall   Short

He deduced that a "factor" for shortness was being passed on, even by tall parents.

Cell science

Meanwhile, scientists were studying cells more and more closely using microscopes. By 1880, they had seen small strands called chromosomes copying themselves inside cells. Soon after that, a German biologist, Wilhelm Roux, suggested it was chromosomes that contained information that passed on features from parents to children.

In the early 1900s, Mendel's work was rediscovered. Scientists realized that his "factors" – renamed "genes" – must be found in chromosomes. It wasn't until 1944 that American scientist Oswald Avery finally found out what chromosomes were made of: a chemical called DNA, short for Deoxyribonucleic Acid.

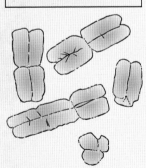

Chromosomes are long strands of DNA found inside the nucleus, or control centre, of a cell.

Unravelling DNA

In the 1950s, two scientists, Francis Crick and James Watson, studied DNA to try to discover its exact shape and structure. Another scientist, Rosalind Franklin, had used a type of X-ray photography to reveal that DNA had a double helix shape, like a ladder twisted in a spiral. Using this fact, and 3-D models of molecules, Watson and Crick finally figured out how DNA worked.

This diagram shows the structure of DNA. The "rungs" of the spiral ladder shape are made of pairs of chemicals called "bases". These chemicals are called adenine, cytosine, guanine and thymine – known as A, C, G and T for short.

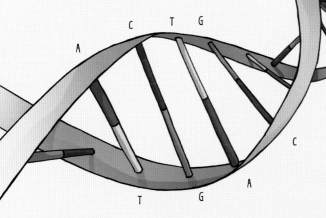

Sections of a chromosome, known as genes, connect in specific patterns that act as a code.

In every DNA chain, chemical A always pairs with T, and C always pairs with G. This means DNA de-coders only need to identify the chemicals on one side of the rung to know what is on the opposite rung.

Selective breeding

Scientists have only recently understood genes and DNA, but people have been working with them for ages.

Long before humans built the first cities and started farming, they tamed and bred wolves to use as hunting companions. In time, ferocious wolves became friendly dogs, and started to take on new shapes.

All dogs today, regardless of their breed, are the same species, and all are directly descended from wolves.

Redesigning life

Now that they understood how DNA worked, biologists and chemists worked together to synthesise acids that could mimic DNA. By the 1970s, a new science was born – genetic engineering.

Teams managed to remove and replace specific genes within bacteria in 1973, without killing them. By 1978, a company named Genentech managed to engineer some bacteria so they could produce useful medicine.

Amazing animals

For centuries scholars and scientists knew little about how animals think, learn and communicate with each other. But in the 1800s, the boom in science and exploration led to a new area of knowledge – ethology, the study of animal behaviour.

c. 350 BC Aristotle

The great ancient Greek philosopher Aristotle was an early animal expert. He was the first to find out a lot of things we know about animals.

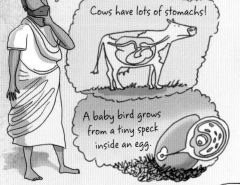

Whales and dolphins are not fish. They're a different kind of animal.

Cows have lots of stomachs!

A baby bird grows from a tiny speck inside an egg.

c. 1880s Magical moth scent

French naturalist Jean-Henri Fabre was one of the first ethologists. He studied and experimented with insects and spiders in the late 1800s.

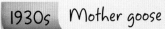

Fabre discovered moths' incredible sense of smell when he caught a female emperor moth.

Male moths from miles around flocked to the female, finding her by her scent.

c. 1900 Pavlov's dogs

Woof! Lunchtime! Slurp!

In the 1890s, Russian scientist Ivan Pavlov was studying dog saliva (spit). He gave dogs food to make them drool saliva for him to collect. He noticed that they could tell when the food was coming and would start drooling ahead of time.

DING!

Slurp...! Hey! Where's my lunch?

Pavlov tried ringing a bell when the food was coming. He found that the dogs learned to drool when they heard the bell, even if there was no food. He had discovered that animals could learn to make a link between a sign and an event.

1930s Mother goose

Konrad Lorenz was an Austrian ethologist famous for his work with baby geese. When the goslings hatched from their eggs, he made sure he was the first thing they saw. They followed him around, thinking he was their mother!

Quack! Mummy!

The goslings "imprinted" the first thing they saw into their brains and remembered it. This would normally be their mother, but Lorenz showed it could be anything – even a box pulled along by a string.

Quack!

1960 Clever chimps

British ethologist Jane Goodall has spent many years studying chimpanzees in the wild. In 1960 she saw chimps stripping the leaves from twigs, then sticking them into termite mounds to catch termites to eat. It was proof that chimps made their own tools.

MUNCH! Delicious!

Until then, scientists didn't know animals made tools. In fact, they thought tool-making was what made humans different from animals. So, they had to rethink what it meant to be human.

1960s Dancing bees

Another Austrian, Karl von Frisch, studied bees in the 1960s. He thought that the "waggle dances" they did in the hive were used to tell other bees how to find patches of tasty flowers. A bee dances to tell the other bees how to reach a food supply it has found.

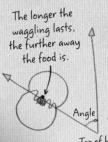

The longer the waggling lasts, the further away the food is.

Angle

Top of hive

Sun

Food

The angle between the dance and the top of the hive tells the bees what direction to fly in compared to the Sun.

Angle

Hive

Von Frisch couldn't prove his theory for sure. But in 2003, UK researchers fixed tiny tracking devices to bees to see where they went – and found that von Frisch was right.

1960s onwards Animal language

Animals communicate in many ways, but do they have language like we do? Scientists are still trying to answer this difficult question.

1967

In 1967 scientists found that vervet monkeys use different calls to warn each other about different dangerous animals.

Like human words, each type of vervet call stands for something:

huh-huh! = eagle
chutter chutter! = snake
bark! = leopard

chutter chutter!

2010s

Bottlenose dolphins talk to each other constantly using whistles, clicks and body language. Sophisticated underwater microphones have recently revealed that they even use unique sounds for names.

In 2011, dolphin researcher Denise Herzing set up an underwater keyboard that can mimic certain dolphin sounds, in the hope of learning to understand just a fraction of their language.

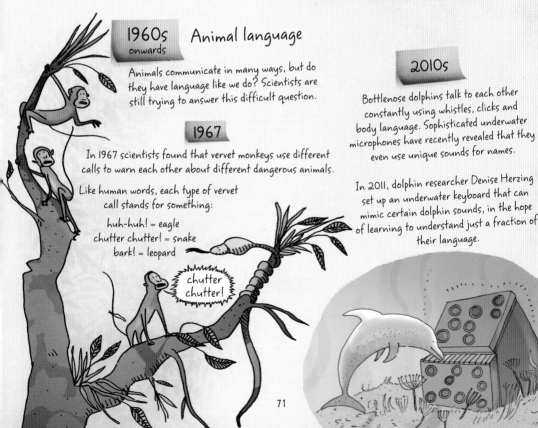

After removing a dead body's organs, the Egyptians would preserve the body and wrap it up to make a mummy.

The organs were buried separately in canopic jars, like these.

Human dissection

Dissecting real human bodies has never been easy. It has often been banned by law, or prevented by religious beliefs.

A few ancient Greeks, such as Herophilos, did dissect humans, but Aristotle and Galen worked with animals such as dogs and baboons instead. In Galen's time, dissection of humans was banned.

Later, doctors in some parts of Europe were allowed to dissect the bodies of criminals who had been sentenced to death. But fewer executions led to graves being robbed to provide more bodies.

Heeelp!

In Scotland in the 1800s, two notorious criminals, Burke and Hare, murdered 17 people to sell their bodies for dissection.

What's inside us?

The earliest people knew that our bodies contain blood, bones, stringy bits and other parts. But discovering how it all worked wasn't easy – especially as you have to dissect people, or cut them up, if you want to study human anatomy (the science of the body)!

Ancient Egyptian anatomy

When wealthy people died in ancient Egypt, their bodies were cut open and their organs carefully removed. The Egyptians knew a lot about body parts and carried out operations. An Egyptian textbook from around 4,000 years ago describes the brain, liver, kidneys and bladder, and shows the heart linked to tubes (the blood vessels).

Galen and the Greeks

From about 400BC, ancient Greeks such as Aristotle used dissection to study body parts. They learned a lot about bones, muscles, and organs such as the heart and kidneys. But they mainly dissected the bodies of monkeys, dogs or pigs, which don't always work like the human body.

The Greeks also thought a healthy body had a balance of four "humours", or fluids: blood, phlegm, black bile and yellow bile – which scientists now know isn't true.

In around 150-200, Galen, a Greek doctor, wrote many books on anatomy. They were translated into Arabic in the 800s, then spread around Europe. For over 1,000 years, ideas about the human body were based mainly on the four humours and animal anatomy.

Ouch!

Blood-letting was a popular medical treatment for many centuries. It was based on the ancient Greek idea that you could have too much blood, and needed to let some out.

Could Galen be wrong?

Around 1540, a Belgian anatomy professor, Andreas Vesalius, was working at the university of Padua in Italy. At this time, most scholars used Galen's books and assumed everything in them was true.

But Vesalius had other ideas. In Padua, the bodies of dead criminals were sent to the university to be dissected – which meant that Vesalius could study them closely. He discovered that Galen hadn't dissected human bodies at all, and that many of his ideas were wrong.

Andreas Vesalius

Nothing more useful could I do but to provide a new description of the totality of the human body.

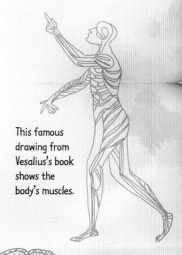

Vesalius's book *On the Structure of the Human Body* caused a big stir and became a bestseller. Vesalius was very proud of it.

A book of the body

To set the record straight, Vesalius paid skilled artists to draw detailed illustrations of the bodies he had dissected. In 1543 he published the drawings in a book, *De Humani Corporis Fabrica (On the Structure of the Human Body)*. Although not completely correct, it was the most detailed description of our insides the world had ever seen.

Some people were angry that Vesalius had dared to challenge the great Galen – but his work set a fashion for close, accurate study of the human body, and paved the way for centuries of new discoveries.

This famous drawing from Vesalius's book shows the body's muscles.

A detailed drawing by Vesalius showing several parts of the human brain

More to find out

As microscopes and the sciences of chemistry and biology became more advanced, anatomists found out – and are still finding out – more and more about what our blood, bones, muscles and organs do. In 2013, a team of surgeons in Belgium discovered previously unknown ligaments in knee joints. Neuroanatomists may never finish piecing together the network of nerves in the brain.

Scientists today are finding out much more than ever before about the human body, using very powerful modern microscopes.

Today we know that coughs and sneezes spread germs that can infect other people. But just 200 years ago, no one really knew how diseases spread.

Germs and disease

Germs are tiny living things that can cause diseases. They're everywhere – in water, air, soil, in houses and on our skin. But, as they're too small to see, it took centuries to realize how germs could make people ill.

Ancient ideas

...certain minute creatures which cannot be seen by the eyes... float in the air and enter the body through the mouth and nose and there cause serious diseases.

Around 2,000 years ago, Roman writer Marcus Terentius Varro guessed how germs work.

As well as the ancient Greek idea that the body contained four "humours" and that having too much of one could make people ill, it was also common to believe that illnesses were caused deliberately by an angry God, or gods. In fact this idea was still widespread until only a few hundred years ago.

But, even in ancient times, some people guessed that diseases could be carried by tiny, invisible creatures.

Germs from nowhere

In the 1600s, people first saw microorganisms (tiny creatures) using microscopes. But they didn't understand where germs came from, or how they lived.

One popular idea – known as "spontaneous generation" – suggested that living creatures could simply appear by themselves, for example in mud or rotting food.

Types of germs
There are several different types of germs.

Protozoa are tiny, single-celled, animal-like creatures.

Malaria protozoan

Bacteria also have only one cell each. They cause many kinds of illnesses and infections.

Cholera bacterium

Viruses are very, very small germs. They have to invade living cells in order to feed and reproduce.

Flu virus

In 1668, Italian doctor Francesco Redi did this experiment to test spontaneous generation. It showed maggots didn't grow out of meat, but arrived from elsewhere. Maggots are actually fly larvae (babies) and hatch from fly eggs.

Redi put meat in an open jar and left it to rot. Maggots soon appeared on the meat.

But if he covered the jar to stop flies getting in, there were no maggots.

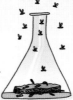

The spread of disease

Gradually people began to see that, like maggots, diseases did not just appear. They were caused by something that could spread from person to person, or live in water or dirt.

In 1847, Hungarian doctor Ignaz Semmelweiss found that if doctors in his maternity hospital washed their hands between treating patients, far fewer became ill. But his discovery was ridiculed at the time.

A few years later, in 1854, an English doctor, John Snow, studied the way cases of cholera, another fatal disease, spread out around a single water pump in London. Something was carrying diseases from place to place and Snow's work showed that it was the water that carried it.

Before Snow's study of cholera, people had thought it was caused by clouds of "bad air" floating around.

Pasteur's proof

Louis Pasteur, a French scientist, brought many of these ideas together in the 1850s and 1860s. He used microscopes and a series of experiments to show that germs do breed and cause diseases, and can spread around in the air, in water and on our bodies.

Pasteur found that germs make milk go off, and that heating the milk kills the germs.

He found the germs that caused anthrax and rabies, and used them to make vaccines (see page 74).

He showed that germs did cause illness in hospitals. Using antiseptic to kill germs kept patients safe.

Pasteur's work caused a revolution in medicine and in everyday life. Today, many medicines are designed to kill disease-causing germs. We know that keeping hospitals clean saves lives. And we heat – or "pasteurize" – foods to kill germs and make the food safe.

Germ or no germ?

Not all diseases are caused by germs. Some types of cancer, genetic diseases such as cystic fibrosis, and many mental illnesses have other causes. But understanding germs has helped scientists to prevent and cure many of the world's major killer diseases, including...

Bubonic plague

Tuberculosis (TB)

Malaria

Cholera

Measles

Most milk and many cheeses are now pasteurized.

Mmmm!

Louis Pasteur

Vaccination

You've probably had at least one vaccination, an injection that protects you from a dangerous disease. But how does it work, and how was it first discovered?

Safe survivors

Smallpox facts

Smallpox was a very dangerous disease caused by a virus, which killed up to a third of people who caught it. It caused pus-filled blisters to form all over the body and face, and people who survived could be left with hundreds of deep scars, or "pock marks".

Smallpox spread from one person to another through coughs and sneezes, saliva, or infected clothes or bedclothes.

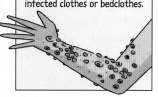

People knew long ago that some diseases can only be caught once. If you get chickenpox, measles or mumps, you probably won't get it it again. Your body becomes "immune" to that disease, meaning it learns how to fight it off.

This also happens with smallpox, a disease that used to kill millions of people. In ancient Greece, those who had already survived smallpox would care for smallpox sufferers, because they didn't catch it again.

Over 2,000 years ago in ancient China and India, people tried to make themselves immune to smallpox. They took a scab or some pus from a person with a mild case of smallpox, and scraped their skin with it. If it worked, this gave them the same mild form of the disease. Afterwards, they were protected from catching smallpox ever again. This process is called inoculation.

Lady Mary Wortley Montagu

Lady Mary Wortley Montagu knew how serious smallpox could be. She had had it herself as a child, and had scars on her face – and her brother had died from it.

On her travels in Turkey, in 1718, Lady Mary Wortley Montagu, an English writer, saw smallpox inoculations taking place. The practice had spread there from the Far East. Seeing how well it worked, Lady Montagu had her own children inoculated. She took her new knowledge with her back to Britain, and gradually, smallpox inoculation began to spread around Europe and North America.

The small-pox, so fatal, and so general amongst us, is here entirely harmless...

Jenner's jab

The problem with inoculation was that it could go wrong, and cause a deadly bout of smallpox. It also helped to spread smallpox around, which was dangerous.

"Mooo!"

Milkmaids were known for their clear complexions. This was because most of them had caught cowpox, so they never caught smallpox.

However, there was another disease, cowpox, that was very like smallpox but much less serious. People who worked with cows knew that no one who caught cowpox from a cow ever seemed to get smallpox.

During the 1700s, several people tried using cowpox to protect against smallpox. But the one who made a difference was Edward Jenner, an English doctor and naturalist. Having heard how cowpox could protect against smallpox, he decided to test it. In 1796, he took some pus from the skin of a milkmaid with cowpox, and scratched it into the arm of his gardener's eight-year-old son, James Phipps.

"Ow!"

Jenner's test wasn't very fair on James Phipps! He survived – but doing a dangerous medical test on a child wouldn't be allowed today.

It worked!

James caught cowpox, as expected, and recovered. Then Jenner tried to infect him with smallpox several times – but James was immune to it. Jenner named the new method "vaccination", from *vacca*, the Latin for cow.

Jenner announced his results and, after a slow start, smallpox vaccination spread around the world. Millions of lives were saved, and by 1980, smallpox was wiped out. Today, smallpox germs only exist in a few science labs.

Vaccinations today

After Jenner, scientists developed vaccines for many more diseases, using dead or weakened disease germs that don't cause serious illness. Today, most of us are vaccinated against measles, polio, TB and several other diseases.

What's in a word?

"Vaccination" and "immunization" both mean using a weakened or milder form of a disease to make you immune. "Inoculation" really means using the same full-strength disease germ that you are protecting against – but doctors also sometimes use it to describe vaccinations, which are also often called "jabs".

Antibiotics

Antibiotics are medicines that kill bacteria. They can be used to help to cure anything from a sore throat or a chest infection, to more serious illnesses, such as meningitis. Famously, they were first found by accident.

Are bacteria bad?

Bacteria are tiny, single-celled living things. Not all bacteria are harmful to humans. Some species live in our bodies and actually do us good, for example by helping us to digest food. But, a few bacteria can cause serious illnesses or dangerous infections, if they get into open wounds.

Escherichia coli or *E. coli* bacteria can be harmless, but some types cause serious food poisoning.

Tuberculosis (TB) bacteria

Staphylococcus aureus bacteria, which can cause acne, meningitis and pneumonia.

Medicines that kill bacteria like these have saved millions of lives.

Modern antibiotic pills

The nose's natural germ-killers

In the First World War (1914-1918), British biologist Alexander Fleming worked as a doctor in army hospitals. He saw countless soldiers die from bacteria-infected battle wounds. Fleming was an expert in bacteria, so after the war he began to look for new bacteria-zapping chemicals. In 1922, he found that a substance in nasal mucus – otherwise known as snot – could kill germs. He named it lysozyme. It wasn't strong enough to use as a medicine, but it showed that living things could make chemicals that killed germs.

A mouldy miracle

A few years later, in 1928, Fleming went on holiday, leaving several test dishes of *Staphylococcus* bacteria growing in his lab. When he came back, a lot of them had gone mouldy, and had to be thrown away. But Fleming noticed that in one dish, a patch of mould had a ring around it where the bacteria didn't grow.

One sometimes finds what one is not looking for...

Fleming was well-known for being messy and not tidying up his lab.

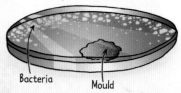

Fleming's test dish was full of bacteria, but it didn't grow near the the patch of mould.

Bacteria   Mould

Penicillin

Fleming realized something in the mould must be killing the bacteria. He studied the mould and extracted the germ-killing chemical, which he named penicillin. In tests, he found it could kill several different types of harmful bacteria. After a few years he stopped experimenting with penicillin, but he kept his results for others to use.

Making a medicine

In 1939, two scientists at Oxford Univeristy, Ernst Chain and Howard Florey, rediscovered Fleming's work. As chemists, they understood molecules and drugs in a way that Fleming, a biologist, did not. They studied the penicillin molecule, and found a new way to extract it and make large amounts of it, so that it could be used to treat infections and illnesses.

When the discovery became widely known, Fleming became very famous, although Howard Florey and Ernst Chain had done just as much important work as he had. In 1945, the Nobel Prize for Medicine was awarded to Fleming, Florey and Chain together.

Antibiotics in action

While Florey and Chain were working with penicillin, the Second World War (1939-1945) began. By the end of the war, in 1945, penicillin was ready for use, and helped to save the lives of thousands of soldiers injured in action.

Since then, we have discovered many more antibiotics made by other moulds and microbes. There are now hundreds of them, all suited to different types of illnesses.

Ernst Chain studied the shape of the penicillin molecule.

Antibiotic resistance

Unfortunately, antibiotics aren't perfect. Some of the bacteria sometimes survive. These super-tough germs then breed, forming a new generation of germs that the antibiotic can't kill. This is called antibiotic resistance, and it is a form of evolution. Carefully taking all your antibiotics helps to wipe out all the bacteria and prevent antibiotic resistance.

1. An antibiotic is used to kill bacteria

2. A few of the bacteria are strong enough to survive.

3. The next generation of germs is resistant to the antibiotic.

Penicillin is still a popular antibiotic, used to treat illnesses such as tonsillitis. It can now be made artificially in the lab, instead of being collected from mould.

Gulp!

Medicines from nature

People have been chewing on herbs to cure illnesses since prehistoric times. Since then, scientists have discovered much more about how some plants, and other living things, can help us fight disease. Even today, scientists are still finding new medicines from the natural world.

Popular remedies that really do work

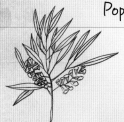

Tea is the most popular herbal drink in the world. It's good for the heart and teeth.

Eating garlic helps to reduce high blood pressure.

Gel from the aloe vera plant helps to repair broken skin.

Honey can soothe coughs and sore throats.

1025 Testing medicines

Persian scholar Ibn Sina (also known as Avicenna) wrote 14 books compiling lists of herbal medicines. More importantly, he described rules for testing whether a medicine actually worked — which not many people did in a scientific way at that time. For example, when testing a medicine, he checked that a sick person didn't get better for some other reason, and that the same medicine worked on different people.

"The effect of the drug must be seen to occur in many cases."

1779 Making pure medicines

Dr. William Withering could not help a patient of his who had dropsy (a heart disease). But the man recovered after taking herbs from a gypsy. She revealed that the key ingredient was a purple foxglove.

Withering was also a keen botanist, so he investigated all kinds of foxgloves. He soon extracted a chemical he called digitalis. Digitalis helps a diseased heart to beat more regularly, and is still used by doctors today.

In fact, foxgloves are very poisonous. So doctors only use digitalis in tiny doses.

1817

Quechua people in the Amazon rainforest had known for hundreds of years that powder made from the bark of the cinchona tree could cure the deadly disease malaria.

A few drops of this and you'll be right as rain.

To investigate this, Frenchmen Pierre-Joseph Pelletier and Joseph-Bienaimé Caventou ground up cinchona bark to find the chemical that was responsible. They called it quinine, and brought the formula for it back to Europe.

1850s Fight the pain

Another Frenchman, Charles Gerhardt, did further research into bark, this time from willow trees. He created acetylsalicylic acid – which was a great painkiller, but he couldn't make it pure enough.

1890s

German drug company Bayer finally found a way to make pure acetylsalicylic acid as a simple pill. They even came up with a catchier name for it – aspirin. Pain and swelling in the body come from substances created by enzymes called COX enzymes. Aspirin works by stopping these enzymes from working.

1906 Magic bullets

In the early 20th century, German Paul Ehrlich was fascinated by the germ theory of disease. He thought that for every germ, there must be a "magic bullet" in nature that could kill it.

In 1906 he used a potion based on arsenic to treat a nasty disease called syphilis. His "magic bullet" idea took off, and doctors around the world began to search for other examples.

1919 Fish find

British chemist Edward Mellanby was determined to cure a bone disease called rickets. He found it wasn't caused by germs, but by a lack of a substance found in cod liver oil. Later scientists named it "vitamin D".

Uuurgh!

During the Second World War, children in Britain all had cod liver oil as part of their food ration.

With help from our little friends we can fight TB and pneumonia.

1939 Soil detective

French-American René Dubos studied tiny microbes that live in soil, looking for germ-zapping chemicals. After 12 years, he finally found that some bacteria make a germ-killing substance called gramicidin. It was one of the first antibiotics.

Hee hee! I can feel them wriggling.

Today Nature quest

Almost all modern pills are based on chemicals first found in a plant or animal. And scientists are still searching the natural world to find new life-saving chemicals. Doctors are also turning back to some ancient remedies, such as using maggots to help wounds heal faster.

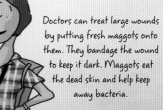

Doctors can treat large wounds by putting fresh maggots onto them. They bandage the wound to keep it dark. Maggots eat the dead skin and help keep away bacteria.

Yum!

Yum...

Dinosaur bones

Millions and millions of years ago, dinosaurs lived on Earth. They were a group of reptiles, related to modern lizards, crocodiles and turtles. Many of them were huge – much bigger than today's biggest land animals, even elephants.

There were many different types of dinosaurs. Some ate plants, and some ate other animals – including other dinosaurs.

Making a fossil

Fossils take many years to form. Here's what happens:

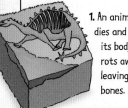

1. An animal dies and its body rots away, leaving the bones.

2. Layers of mud collect on top (especially if the bones are at the bottom of the sea). The layers get squashed down and harden into rock.

3. Water in the rock slowly dissolves the bone, leaving a bone-shaped space. Dissolved minerals gradually collect in the space, creating a bone shape made from stone.

Dragons and monsters

Dinosaurs died out 65 million years ago, but many of their bones were fossilized – trapped under layers of mud and rock, and gradually replaced with minerals. Early people probably found these huge stony bones in the ground, and saw that they resembled enormous lizard-like creatures. This may explain why many cultures have myths and legends about scary monsters and lizard-shaped dragons.

The giant's leg bone

People didn't really begin to study dinosaur fossils in a scientific way until the 1600s. Even then, they didn't know what they were. In 1677, English naturalist Robert Plot included a drawing of a huge fossil femur (thigh bone) in one of his books. He thought it might have come from an elephant, brought to England by the Romans – or that it might be the leg bone of a human giant.

The bone shown in Robert Plot's book was the lower end of a femur. It looked like this:

The whole femur would have been about 1m (over 3 feet) long...

...and if it had come from a giant human, he or she would have been about 4.2m (14 feet) tall.

Seems unlikely...

Finding fossils

By 1800, fossils were fashionable. Mary Anning was a famous fossil finder who collected fossils on the beach at Lyme Regis, England, to sell to tourists and naturalists. From the age of 12, she discovered many important fossils.

People were now starting to piece together prehistoric creatures and give them names. In 1822, Mary Ann Mantell found a large fossil tooth. Her husband, Gideon Mantell, thought it looked like an iguana's tooth. After finding several other teeth, he decided they must come from a giant reptile, which he called *Iguanodon* ("iguana-tooth"). It was the first dinosaur to be named.

Around the same time, geologist William Buckland studied several large bones dug up in England. He believed that these bones, along with the femur from Robert Plot's book, belonged to another giant reptile. He called it *Megalosaurus*, meaning "big lizard".

The terrible lizards

But what were all these creatures? At first, people thought they were just extra-large versions of today's reptiles. But Richard Owen, head of London's Natural History Museum, disagreed. In 1841 he decided that the fossilized giant lizards belonged in their own special group. He gave it a name – the *Dinosauria*, or dinosaurs. It comes from two Greek words, *deinos*, meaning "terrible", and *saurus*, meaning "lizard". (The swimming and flying reptiles, such as *plesiosaurs* and *pterodactyls*, are not true dinosaurs, but are related to them.)

Since then, scientists have found and named hundreds of new types of dinosaurs – and they are still finding more.

Mary Anning found whole fossil skeletons of an *ichthyosaur* (a prehistoric sea reptile), a *plesiosaur* and a *pterodactyl*.

A *plesiosaur* was a prehistoric swimming reptile with flippers and a long neck.

A *pterodactyl* was a huge flying reptile. It could glide along on wings made from skin, like a bat's.

30cm (12 inches)

This is one of the *iguanodon* teeth studied by Dr Gideon Mantell.

0cm (0 inches)

Bones from one of the biggest dinosaurs ever, *Argentinosaurus*, were first discovered in 1993. Experts think it may have been as long as 27m (90 feet).

The Burgess Shale

If it's hard to imagine what life was like in ancient Greece — or even in Victorian times — then what about 500 million years ago? In 1909, a stunning fossil find revealed a world of amazing and bizarre ancient animals.

Who was Walcott?

Charles Doolittle Walcott was born in New York, USA, in 1850. As a teenager he was very interested in nature and fossils. He became a fossil-hunter, finding fossils to sell to museums. This led to a job as an assistant to paleontologist (fossil scientist) James Hall. Eventually, Walcott became head of the US Geological Survey, and then secretary — or boss — of the Smithsonian Institution museum and research centre.

Fossil discovery

In 1909, Charles Doolittle Walcott, a leading US fossil expert, went on a fossil-hunting trip to the area around Banff in Canada. On a mountain trail, he stumbled across a slab of rock full of beautiful, brilliantly preserved fossils of *Phyllopoda* — ancient water fleas.

Walcott knew the slab must have fallen from further up the mountain, so he set out to find the rock it had come from. He discovered an area of shale — fine-grained rock made from layers of flattened mud. In it were thousands of astonishing sea, or marine, fossils, dating from the Middle Cambrian period, 500-512 million years ago. Walcott named it the Burgess Shale, after nearby Mount Burgess.

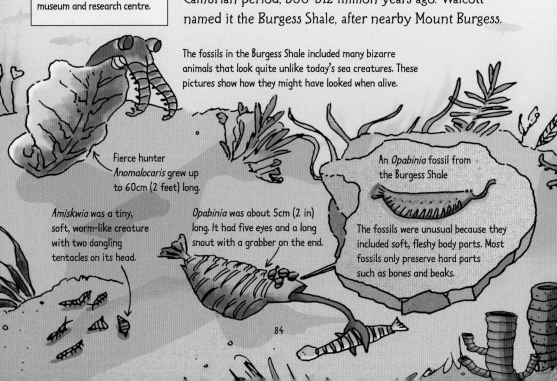

The fossils in the Burgess Shale included many bizarre animals that look quite unlike today's sea creatures. These pictures show how they might have looked when alive.

Fierce hunter *Anomalocaris* grew up to 60cm (2 feet) long.

Amiskwia was a tiny, soft, worm-like creature with two dangling tentacles on its head.

Opabinia was about 5cm (2 in) long. It had five eyes and a long snout with a grabber on the end.

An *Opabinia* fossil from the Burgess Shale

The fossils were unusual because they included soft, fleshy body parts. Most fossils only preserve hard parts such as bones and beaks.

Sorting and studying

Over the next 15 years, Walcott, with his sons Sidney and Stuart, returned to the site many times and collected over 65,000 fossils. He took them to his workplace, the Smithsonian Institution in Washington D.C. But he was so busy, they sat in dusty old drawers for more than 50 years.

Then, in the 1960s, long after Walcott's death, British fossil scientist Harry B. Whittington, and his students Derek Briggs and Simon Conway Morris, decided to study the fossils carefully to see what kinds of creatures they were.

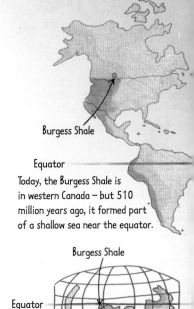

Burgess Shale

Equator

Today, the Burgess Shale is in western Canada – but 510 million years ago, it formed part of a shallow sea near the equator.

Burgess Shale

Equator

Strange beasts

To the scientists' surprise, many of the Burgess Shale fossils did not look like any type of creature ever discovered before. Until then, people assumed that in Cambrian times, living things were quite simple, and that there were fewer types of animals than there are today. But, the Burgess Shale revealed that there were animal families that don't even exist now, and that life then was incredibly complex.

How did it happen?

Why were the Burgess Shale fossils so perfectly preserved? Most fossils form when dead creatures are gradually covered by silt sinking onto the seabed. But recent studies show that the Burgess Shale formed when a series of sudden mudslides fell into the shallow sea, burying the animals alive and keeping them whole.

Legs or spines?

One of the strangest animals found in the Burgess Shale is the odd-looking *Hallucigenia*. When he first studied it in the 1960s, Simon Conway Morris decided it walked on its pointy spines, using its tentacles to catch food like this:

But in the 1990s, two other scientists, Lars Ramskold and Hou Xianguang, said *Hallucigenia* was really the other way up, with the tentacles used for walking and the spines for protection.

The crustacean *Waptia* was related to modern shrimps.

Impact Earth

What if a massive asteroid, 10km (6 miles) across, came zooming through space and smashed into our planet, turning the sky dark and wiping out thousands of species of living things? Well, it's actually already happened.

What is an asteroid?

An asteroid is a lump of rock or metal that orbits around the Sun. The word asteroid means "star-like", but asteroids are actually more like tiny planets, ranging from a few metres to over 900 km across. There are thousands of asteroids, and most are nowhere near our planet. But sometimes, we get in the way of a hurtling asteroid and it hits the Earth. Asteroid impacts as big as the one at Yucatan are very rare, but one day, another huge asteroid could come our way.

Mystery crater

In the late 1970s, Glen Penfield, a geologist working for an oil company, was searching for good places to drill for oil in the sea off the coast of Mexico. As he studied maps that had been made of the area, he found, to his surprise, that the pattern of rocks underground and under the seabed formed a perfect ring shape, over 180km (110 miles) across. It was half in the sea and half on land, on the northern coast of Mexico's Yucatan Peninsula.

Penfield saw that the ring looked like an impact crater – the shape made by a large object crashing into the ground. But to make a crater this big, the object must have been huge.

Asteroid evidence

Meanwhile, two American scientists, Luis Alvarez and his son Walter Alvarez, had found the rare element iridium in a layer of 65-million-year-old rocks in Gubbio, Italy. Iridium is found in asteroids, and the Alvarezes thought that the iridium layer might have been left by a big asteroid hitting the Earth, shattering and spreading dust around the globe. Other scientists found evidence of more 65-million-year-old iridium layers in other parts of the world. But, if an asteroid had hit, where was the crater?

When the asteroid landed, the area it hit was a shallow sea. The impact threw out vast amounts of rock and mud to made a huge crater, which was immediately filled in with seawater.

84

Adding it all up

Although Penfield announced his discovery in 1981, it took over 10 years for the different scientists to collect all the facts together. Finally, in the 1990s, tests on the rocks at Yucatan showed the crater was about 65 million years old, and that it was made by a massive asteroid at least 10km (6 miles) wide.

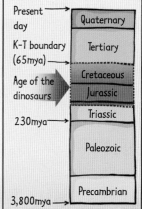

I've found a massive crater... but what caused it?

A massive asteroid must have landed... but where?

Dinosaur disaster?

An asteroid this big would have had an impact all over the world (including Italy) especially affecting Earth's living things. As well as causing vast tsunamis and floods, it would have thrown huge amounts of dust and ash into orbit, blocking out the sunlight and killing plants. Without plants to eat, many animals would have died.

Fossils do show that, 65 million years ago, many species of living things — including the last of the dinosaurs — became extinct. This big change in life on Earth is usually called the "K-T boundary" — the boundary, or dividing line, between the Cretaceous (K) and Tertiary (T) periods of the Earth's history (see right). Most scientists agreed that it must have been the Yucatan asteroid that wiped out the dinosaurs, along with many other prehistoric creatures.

But, some experts now think that may not be true after all. They say the asteroid may have hit slightly earlier than 65 million years ago — and that, as the dinosaurs took millions of years to die out, there must have been other causes. One theory is that there was a series of massive volcanic eruptions, which were even more disastrous than the asteroid.

The dinosaur years

When the dinosaurs died out 65 million years ago, they had lived on Earth for ages and ages. They first appeared 230 million years ago (mya) during the Triassic period. Not all species of dinosaurs lived at the same time. When the asteroid landed, earlier dinosaurs such as *Plateosaurus* and *Diplodocus* were already extinct. The dinosaurs that were still around included *Tyrannosaurus rex* and *Triceratops*.

Present day →	Quaternary
K-T boundary (65mya) →	Tertiary
	Cretaceous
Age of the dinosaurs	Jurassic
230mya →	Triassic
	Paleozoic
3,800mya →	Precambrian

Oh no. Not again...

What's the matter?

Exactly!

More to discover

If you think scientists have all the answers, you're wrong! There are many scientific puzzles that are still unsolved. And they just happen to be the biggest questions of all — things like the nature of time, matter, life, gravity and thought.

We are all made of matter, and so is everything we can touch and hold. So it's a bit weird that we don't know what it is!

The mystery of matter

Matter is the stuff that makes up the objects and materials around us. Scientists already know a lot about matter. They know it's made up of tiny atoms, which are made of tinier parts such as protons and neutrons. And these are made of even tinier parts, called fermions and bosons.

But what are those made of? Are they even made of 'things' at all? No one knows. One idea, called string theory, says that at a very, very small scale, everything is made of tiny mathematical building blocks called strings. But, as they are SO small, it's impossible to see them or test the theory.

Science spats

When scientists discover new things, they generally all agree on them. But there are some topics that they argue about — especially tough problems like the ones on these pages. Scientists publish their results and theories in scientific journals (similar to magazines), and debate their ideas there.

You're late.

That's impossible!

They may also meet up at conferences, and have arguments face-to-face!

About time

We have to deal with time constantly, so we feel as if we know what it is. But if you try to explain it, it's not easy.

There are two main ideas about time. One says that it is a real part of the universe, and is connected to other parts of reality, such as space and motion. Other thinkers say that time isn't real. It's just an illusion — our way of making sense of the way things seem to happen in a sequence. It's very hard to prove either of these theories — so the truth about time is still a puzzle.

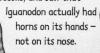

You're upside-down, not me!

Grasping gravity

In everyday life, gravity feels like a force that pulls us down to the ground. In fact, all matter has gravity – a force that makes objects pull toward each other. But why – and how? Is gravity a pulling force that reaches out across space to make objects move? If so, how does it do that? Or does matter make space and time curve, so that objects are drawn together, as Einstein said (see page 37)? Ideas to do with gravity are very hard to understand, and scientists haven't yet reached an agreement.

Thinking and the brain

You know what thoughts and feelings are, and when you have them. In other words, you have "consciousness". You are conscious, or aware, of your self and your thoughts.

But how does that happen? How can electrical signals jumping between brain cells add up to conscious thoughts, experiences and a "self"? Some scientists say something in the brain makes us conscious. Others say it's just an illusion, caused by our brains making a constant series of decisions.

Understanding everything!

Scientists often find that their theories about time, matter and so on don't fit together. If one is right, another must be wrong. What they really want is a "Theory of Everything" – one idea that explains everything in the universe. Will they ever find it? Perhaps, if you become a scientist, you could be the one to solve this problem.

Of course, gravity doesn't actually pull you down – it just pulls you towards the Earth, whichever way up you are. As you are an object, you pull very slightly on the Earth too.

Changing facts

Science is made of facts – but we can only decide what a fact is by looking at the evidence, and trying to make sense of it. As time goes on, scientists find new evidence, and new ways to look at things – so the "facts" change. One day, we may find new answers to the puzzles on these pages – and some of the facts on the other pages of this book will change, too.

When Iguanodon fossils were first discovered, scientists decided a horn-shaped bone fitted on the dinosaur's nose. Later, other scientists found more fossils, and saw that Iguanodon actually had horns on its hands – not on its nose.

Horn-shaped thumb bone

What's your theory on?

Everything.

Ooooh...

Timeline of scientific discoveries

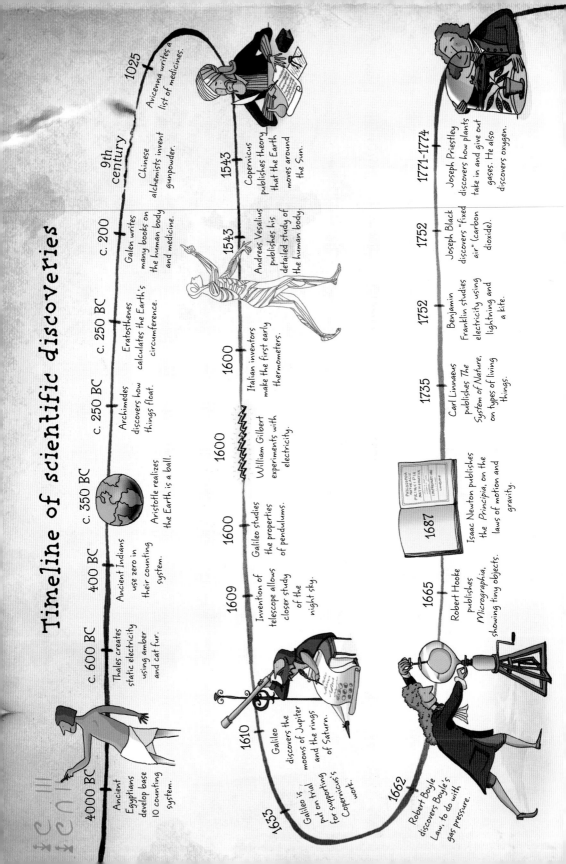

4000 BC
Ancient Egyptians develop base 10 counting system.

c. 600 BC
Thales creates static electricity using amber and cat fur.

400 BC
Ancient Indians use zero in their counting system.

c. 350 BC
Aristotle realizes the Earth is a ball.

c. 250 BC
Archimedes discovers how things float.

c. 250 BC
Eratosthenes calculates the Earth's circumference.

c. 200
Galen writes many books on the human body and medicine.

9th century
Chinese alchemists invent gunpowder.

1025
Avicenna writes a list of medicines.

1543
Copernicus publishes theory that the Earth moves around the Sun.

1543
Andreas Vesalius publishes his detailed study of the human body.

1600
Italian inventors make the first early thermometers.

1600
William Gilbert experiments with electricity.

1600
Galileo studies the properties of pendulums.

1609
Invention of telescope allows closer study of the night sky.

1610
Galileo discovers the moons of Jupiter and the rings of Saturn.

1633
Galileo is put on trial for supporting Copernicus's work.

1662
Robert Boyle discovers Boyle's Law, to do with gas pressure.

1665
Robert Hooke publishes Micrographia, showing tiny objects.

1687
Isaac Newton publishes the Principia, on the laws of motion and gravity.

1735
Carl Linnaeus publishes The System of Nature, on types of living things.

1752
Benjamin Franklin studies electricity using lightning and a kite.

1752
Joseph Black discovers "fixed air" (carbon dioxide).

1771-1774
Joseph Priestley discovers how plants take in and give out gases. He also discovers oxygen.

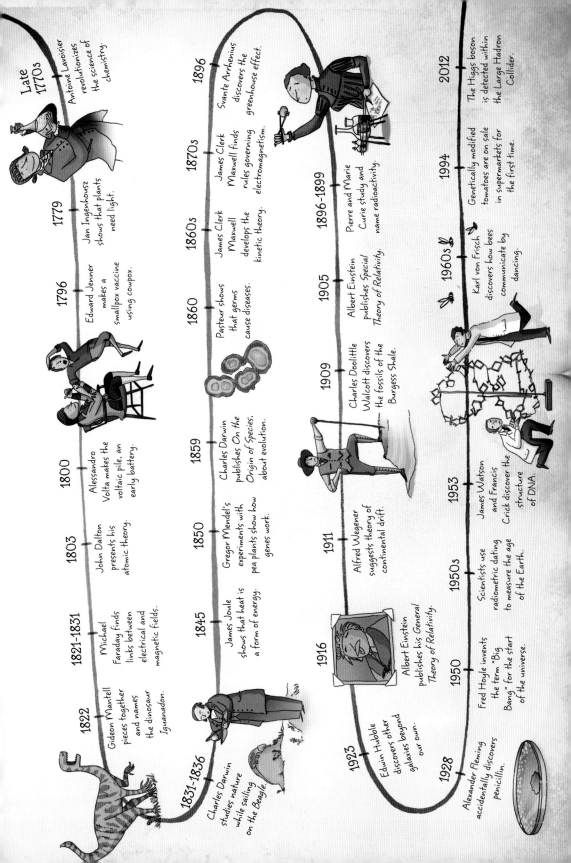

Late 1770s — Antoine Lavoisier revolutionizes the science of chemistry.

1779 — Jan Ingenhousz shows that plants need light.

1796 — Edward Jenner makes a smallpox vaccine using cowpox.

1800 — Alessandro Volta makes the voltaic pile, an early battery.

1803 — John Dalton presents his atomic theory.

1821–1831 — Michael Faraday finds links between electrical and magnetic fields.

1822 — Gideon Mantell pieces together and names the dinosaur Iguanadon.

1831–1836 — Charles Darwin studies nature while sailing on the Beagle.

1845 — James Joule shows that heat is a form of energy.

1850 — Gregor Mendel's experiments with pea plants show how genes work.

1859 — Charles Darwin publishes On The Origin of Species, about evolution.

1860 — Pasteur shows that germs cause diseases.

1860s — James Clerk Maxwell develops the kinetic theory.

1870s — James Clerk Maxwell finds rules governing electromagnetism.

1896 — Svante Arrhenius discovers the greenhouse effect.

1896–1899 — Pierre and Marie Curie study and name radioactivity.

1905 — Albert Einstein publishes Special Theory of Relativity.

1909 — Charles Doolittle Walcott discovers the fossils of the Burgess Shale.

1911 — Alfred Wegener suggests theory of continental drift.

1916 — Albert Einstein publishes his General Theory of Relativity.

1923 — Edwin Hubble discovers other galaxies beyond our own.

1928 — Alexander Fleming accidentally discovers penicillin.

1950 — Fred Hoyle invents the term "Big Bang" for the start of the universe.

1950s — Scientists use radiometric dating to measure the age of the Earth.

1953 — James Watson and Francis Crick discover the structure of DNA.

1960s — Karl von Frisch discovers how bees communicate by dancing.

1994 — Genetically modified tomatoes are on sale in supermarkets for the first time.

2012 — The Higgs boson is detected within the Large Hadron Collider.

Glossary

alchemy An early form of chemistry that involved magic and secret codes.

anatomy The study of the human body.

antibiotics Anti-bacterial medicines made from moulds or other microorganisms.

asteroid A lump of rock orbiting the Sun.

astronomer A scientist who studies space, planets and stars.

atoms Tiny particles that matter is made of.

bacteria Microscopic living things that can sometimes cause illness.

billion A thousand million or 1,000,000,000.

black hole An infinitely small, dense point in space that sucks in matter and light.

boson A type of fundamental energy particle that provides the forces to allow atoms to hold together.

botany The scientific study of plants.

cells Tiny units that make up living things.

chromosomes Strings of DNA found inside the cells of living things.

circumference The distance all the way around the edge of a circle or sphere.

classification Sorting living things (or other things) into groups and types.

composite number A non-prime number.

compound A substance made up of different atoms, bonded into molecules.

consciousness Our awareness of our own thoughts and feelings.

constellation A group of stars that appear to us to form a pattern.

continental drift The gradual movement of the continents around the globe.

crater A hole created by the impact of a meteor or asteroid.

density The amount of matter in a substance compared to its volume.

diameter The distance across the middle of a circle or sphere.

dissection Cutting plants or animals open to study their insides.

DNA (short for Deoxyribonucleic Acid) Double spiral ladder-shaped molecule that genes are made of.

dwarf planet A type of small planet.

earthforms Shapes and features of land, such as mountains or cliffs.

electron A tiny charged particle that speeds around the nucleus of an atom.

electromagnetism A form of energy that travels in waves.

element The simplest type of chemical.

energy The power to do work or make things happen.

ethology The study of animal behaviour.

evolution The way species of living things change over time.

extinct An extinct species is one that has died out and no longer exists.

extrasolar planet A planet outside our own Solar System.

fermion A type of fundamental energy particle that forms in groups to make matter.

fossil The shape of a living thing or its remains, preserved inside rock.

friction A force that slows objects down when they drag or rub against each other.

genes Sequences of DNA that hold coded information for building body parts.

germs Small living things, such as bacteria and viruses, that cause illness.

glacier A river of solid ice that gradually moves downhill.

global warming An increase in the Earth's temperature caused by the greenhouse effect.

greenhouse effect Warming of the Earth caused by a build-up of greenhouse gases.

greenhouse gas A gas in the Earth's atmosphere, such as carbon dioxide, that reflects heat back to the Earth.

heliocentricity The theory that the Earth and other planets orbit around the Sun.

humours Four types of imaginary fluid that people once thought controlled health and sickness in the body.

ice age An unusually cold period in the Earth's history.

infinity An endless amount or number.

kinetic theory A theory that explains heat as increased motion of the atoms or molecules in a substance.

lava Melted rock from inside the Earth flowing out of the ground.

light year The distance that light travels in a year – about 9.5 trillion km or 5.9 trillion miles.

lunar To do with our moon.

matter The stuff that all objects and materials are made of.

microorganism Tiny living thing.

million A thousand thousand or 1,000,000.

mitosis The process by which a cell divides into two to make new cells.

molecule The smallest possible particle of a compound, made of atoms joined together.

multiverse A possible collection of many different universes.

naturalist A scientist who studies the natural world, animals and plants.

nucleus The central part of a cell or an atom.

orbit To circle around another object.

paleontologist A scientist who studies fossils.

pasteurize To heat milk or other foods to kill germs and make them safe.

photon A small packet of light energy.

photosynthesis The process plants use to make food using sunlight, water and carbon dioxide gas.

planet A large sphere of rock orbiting a star, such as the Sun.

prime number A number that can only be divided by itself and 1.

primeval atom A theoretical solid ball of matter from which everything in the universe expanded.

protozoa A very small living thing that can cause diseases.

radioactivity A harmful form of energy given off by some substances.

radiometric dating Using a radioactive reading to tell the age of something.

relativity A theory that describes the structure of space and time.

Solar System Our Sun and the planets and other objects that orbit around it.

species A type of living thing.

theorem A statement in mathematics that can be proved by mathematical rules.

trillion A million million or 1,000,000,000,000.

universe A name for everything that exists and all of space and time.

X-ray A type of electromagnetic wave with a wavelength longer than visible light.

virus A tiny creature that can cause diseases when it invades body cells.

wavelength The distance from one point on a wave to the same point on the next wave.

Index

Additional design by Ian McNee. Art director: Mary Cartwright.

This edition first published in 2014 by Usborne Publishing Ltd., Usborne House, 83-85 Saffron Hill, London EC1N 8RT, England. www.usborne.com Copyright © 2014, 2008 Usborne Publishing Ltd.